Cute Supermarket Dot To Dot Coloring Book For Kid

Fun Activities To Learn New Vocabulary

Copyright © 2020

All rights reserved. This book or any portion thereof may not be reproduced or used in any manner whatsoever without the express written permission of the publisher except for the use of brief quotations in a book review.

Any references to historical events, real people or real places are used fictitiously. Names, characters, and places are products of the author's imagination.

Printed in the United States of America

First Printing, 2020

ISBN 979-8654835390

Apple

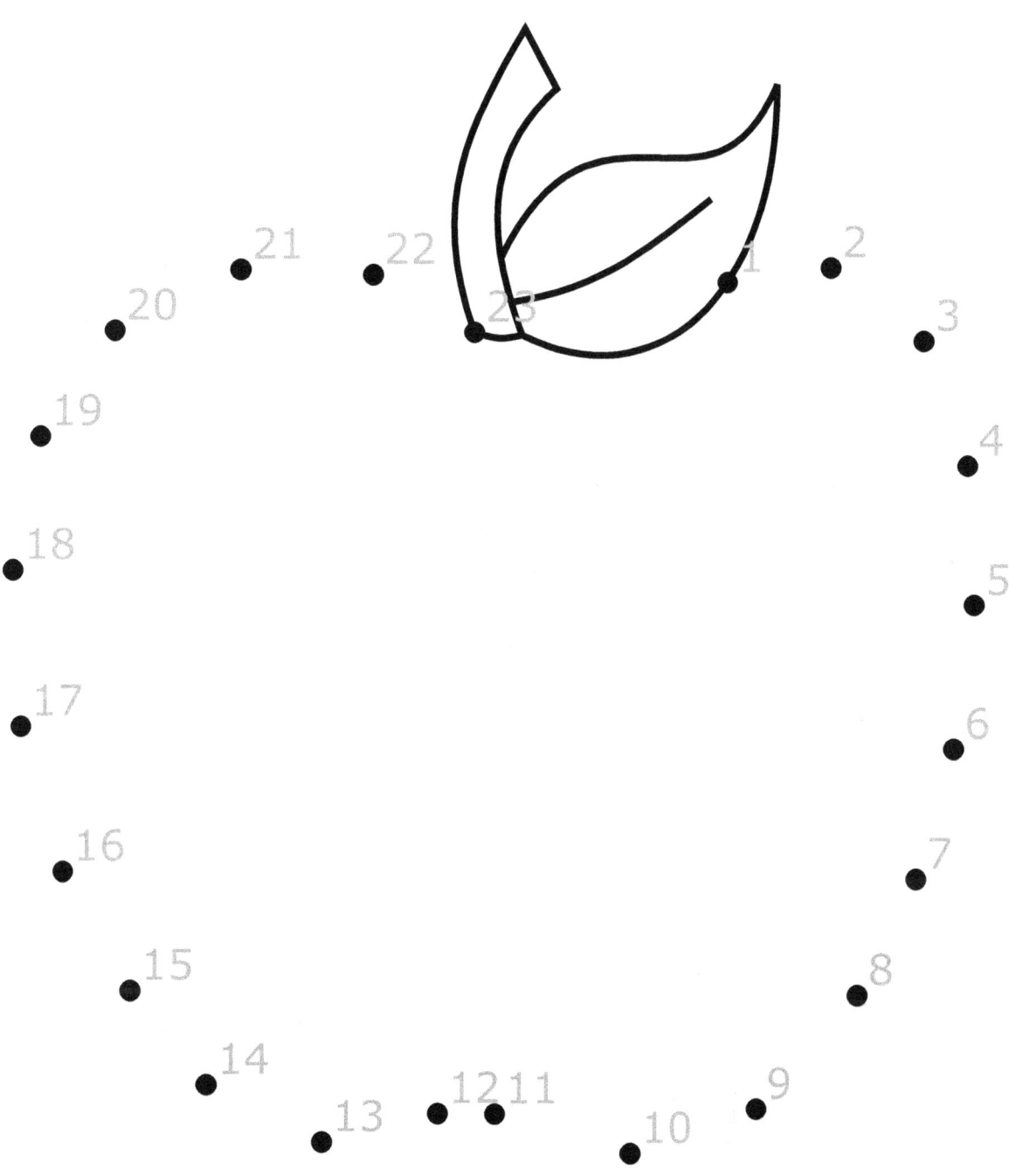

Banana

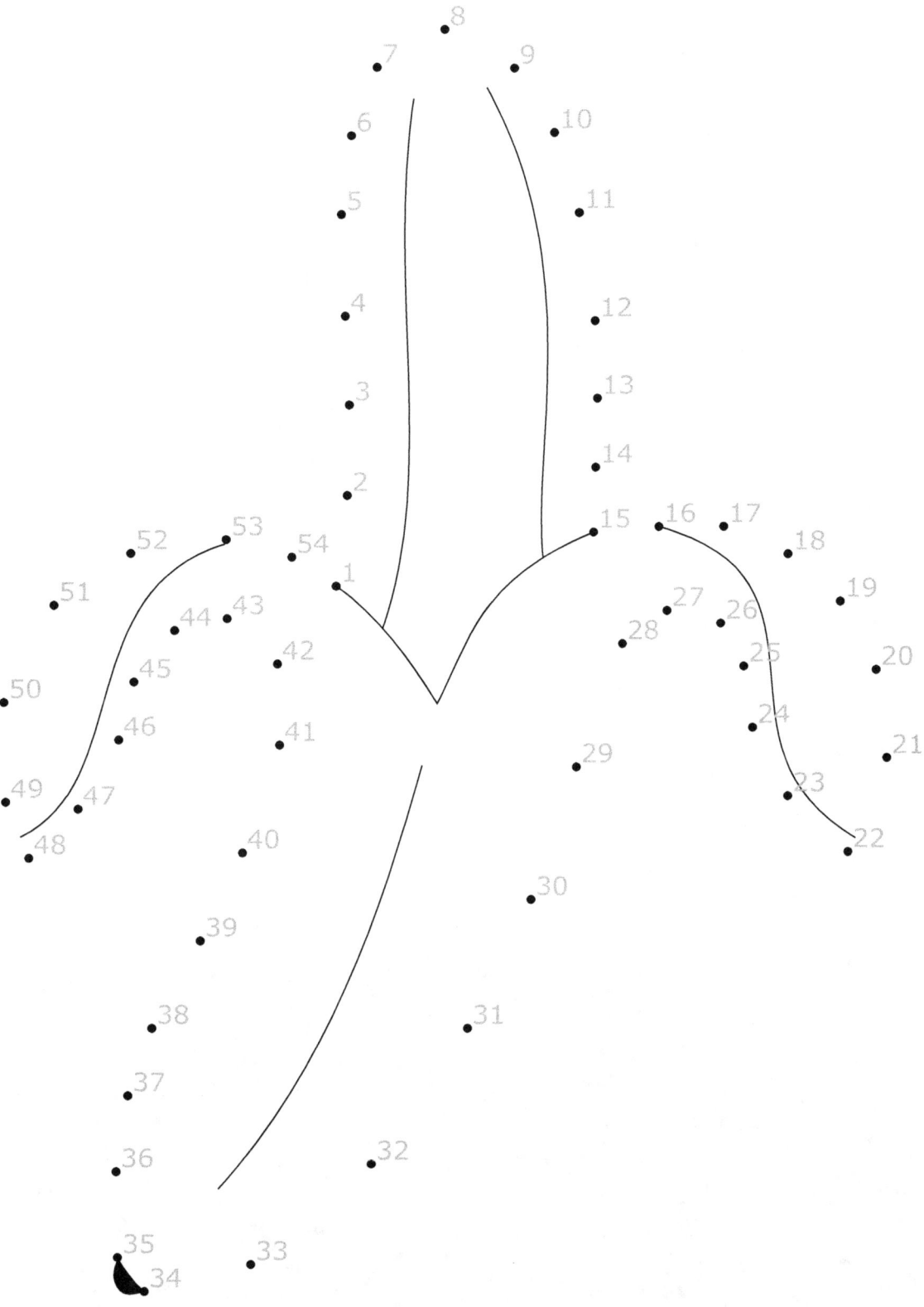

Basket

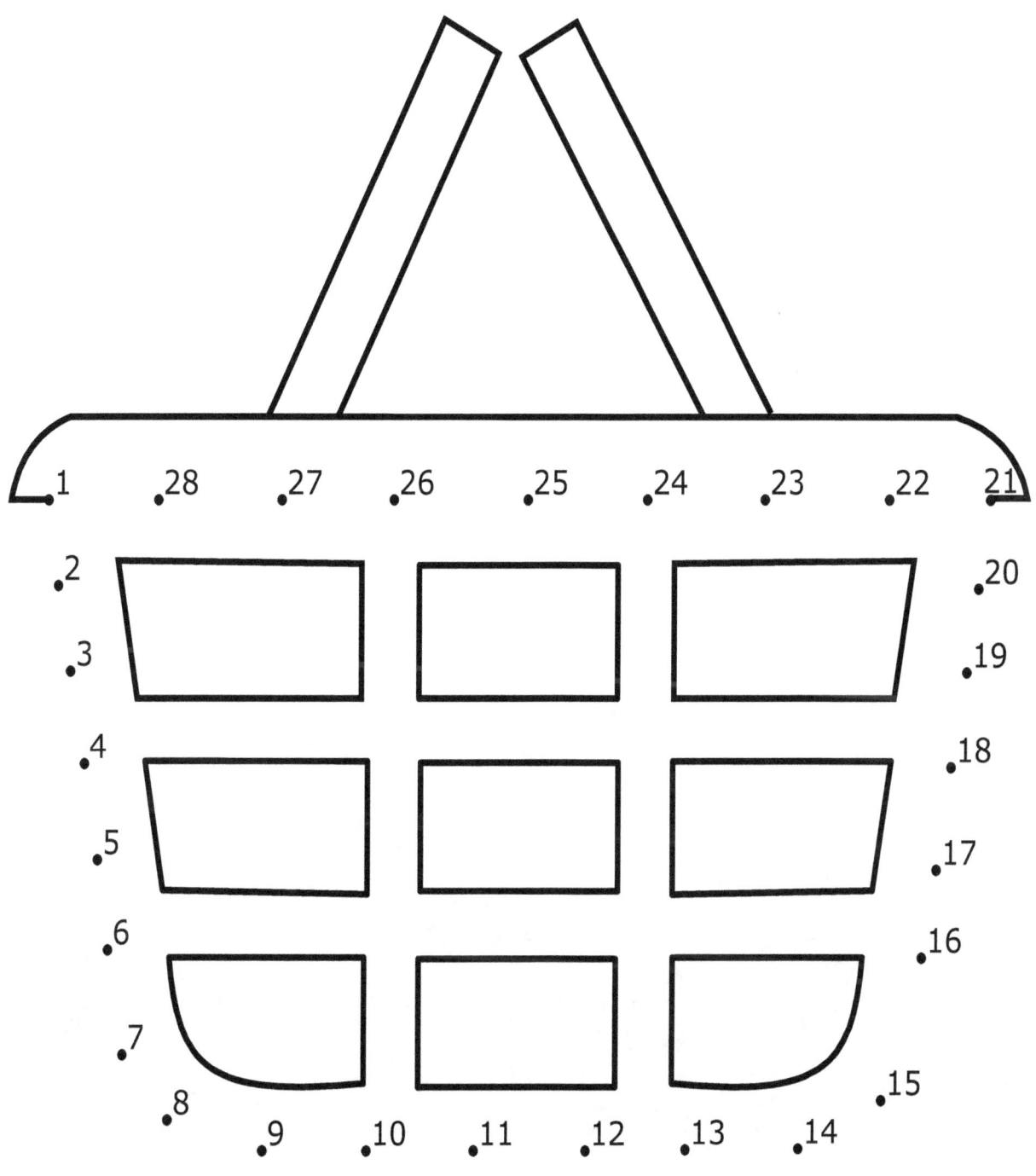

Battery

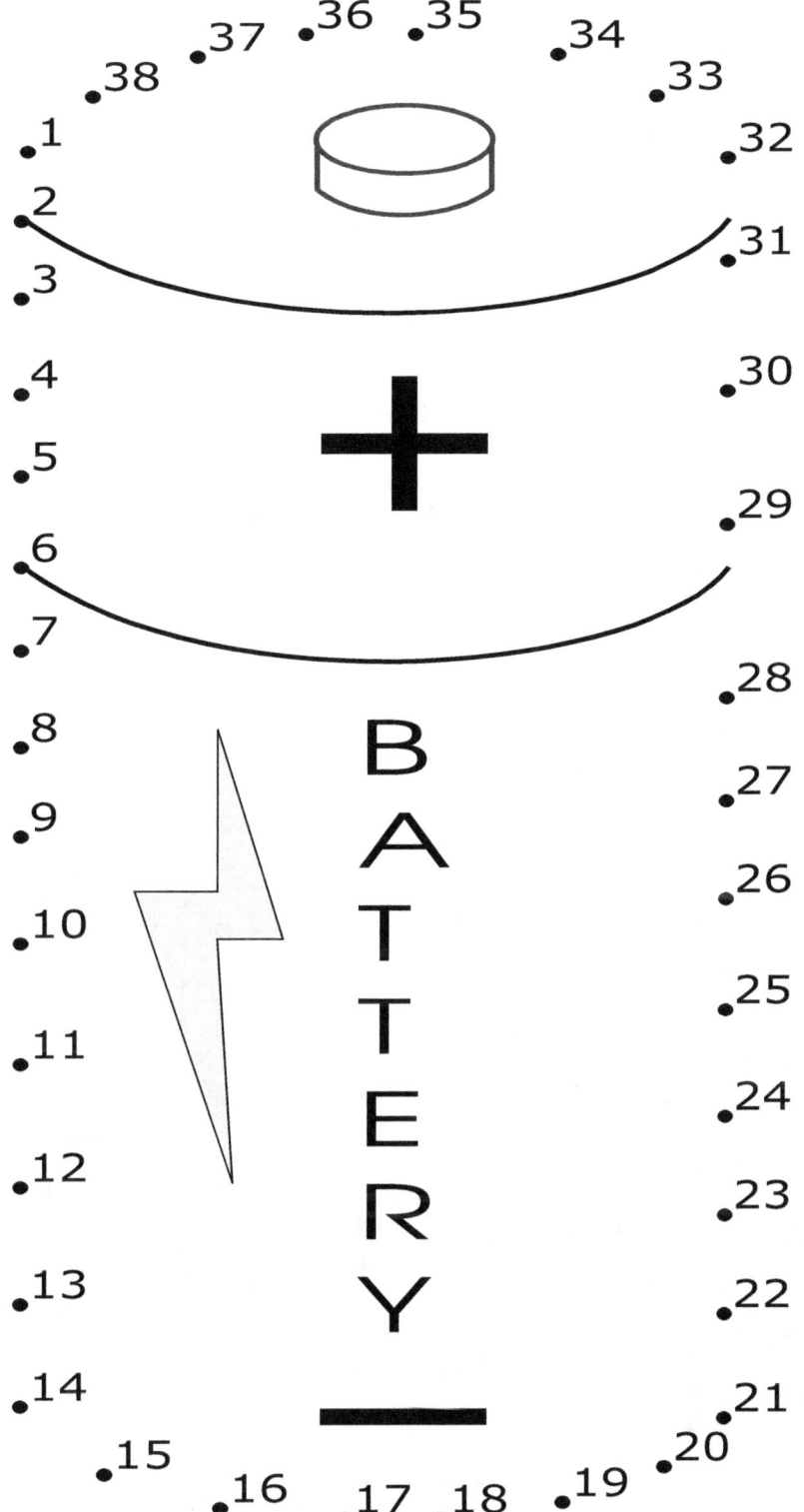

Beef

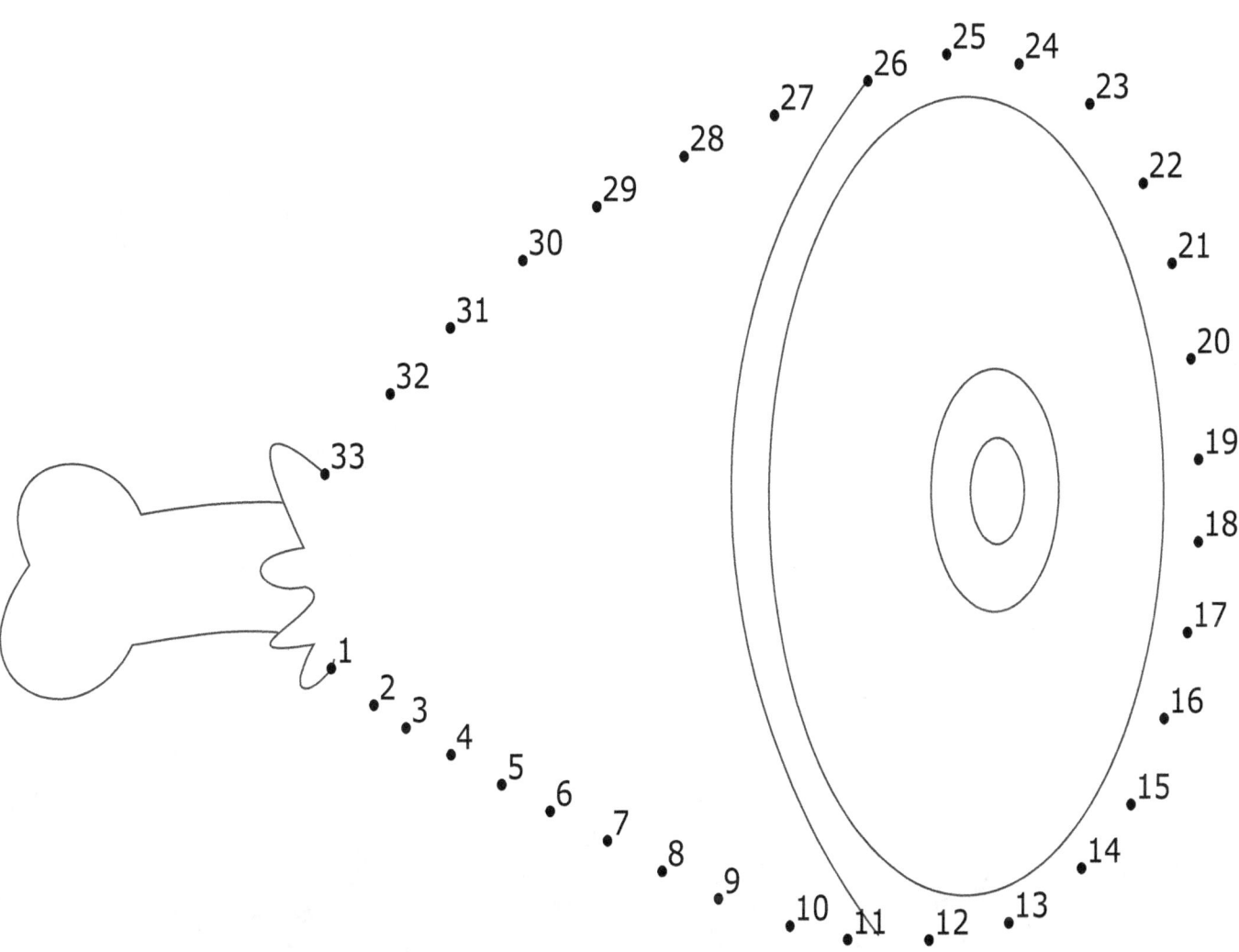

Bread

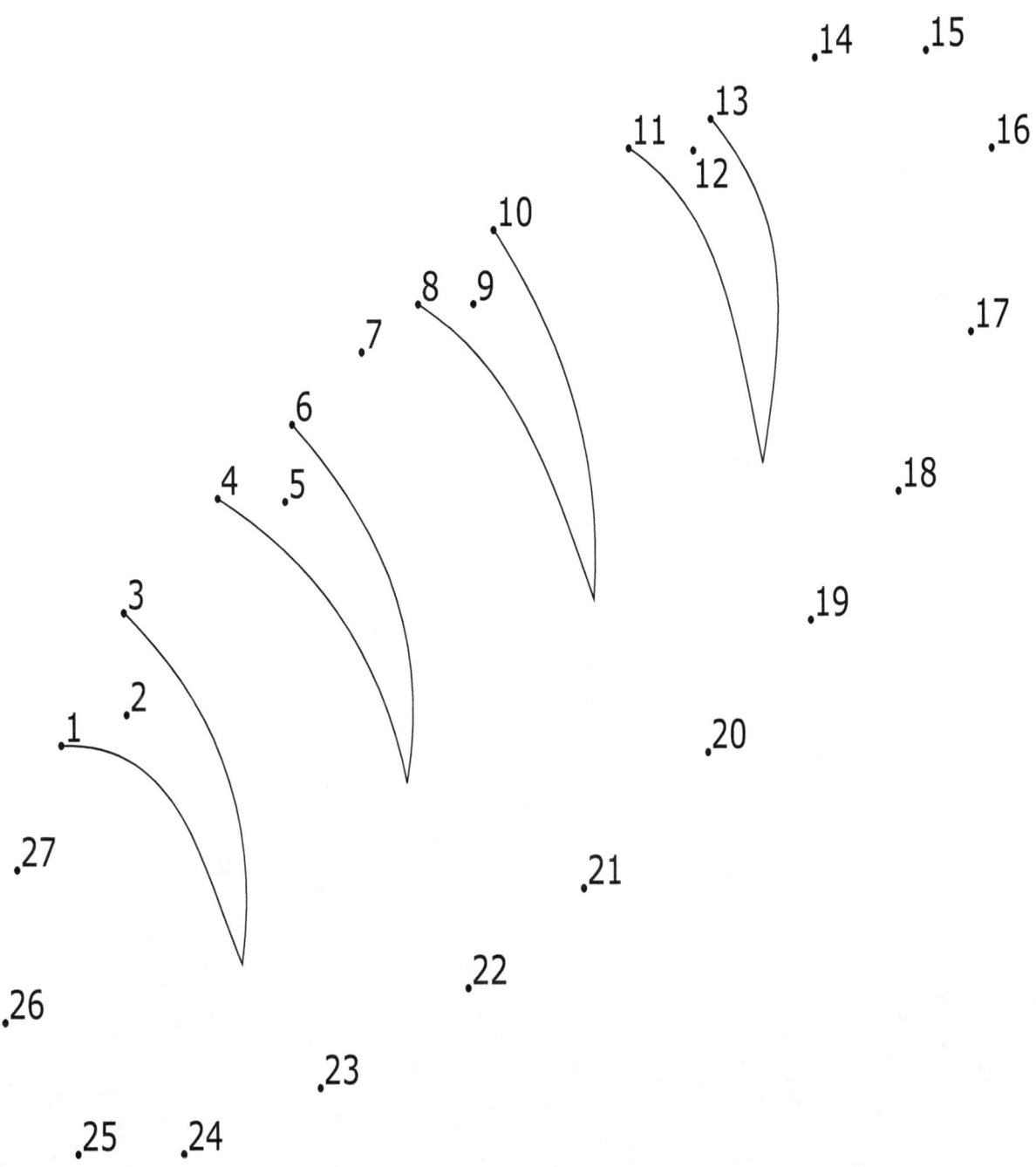

Butter

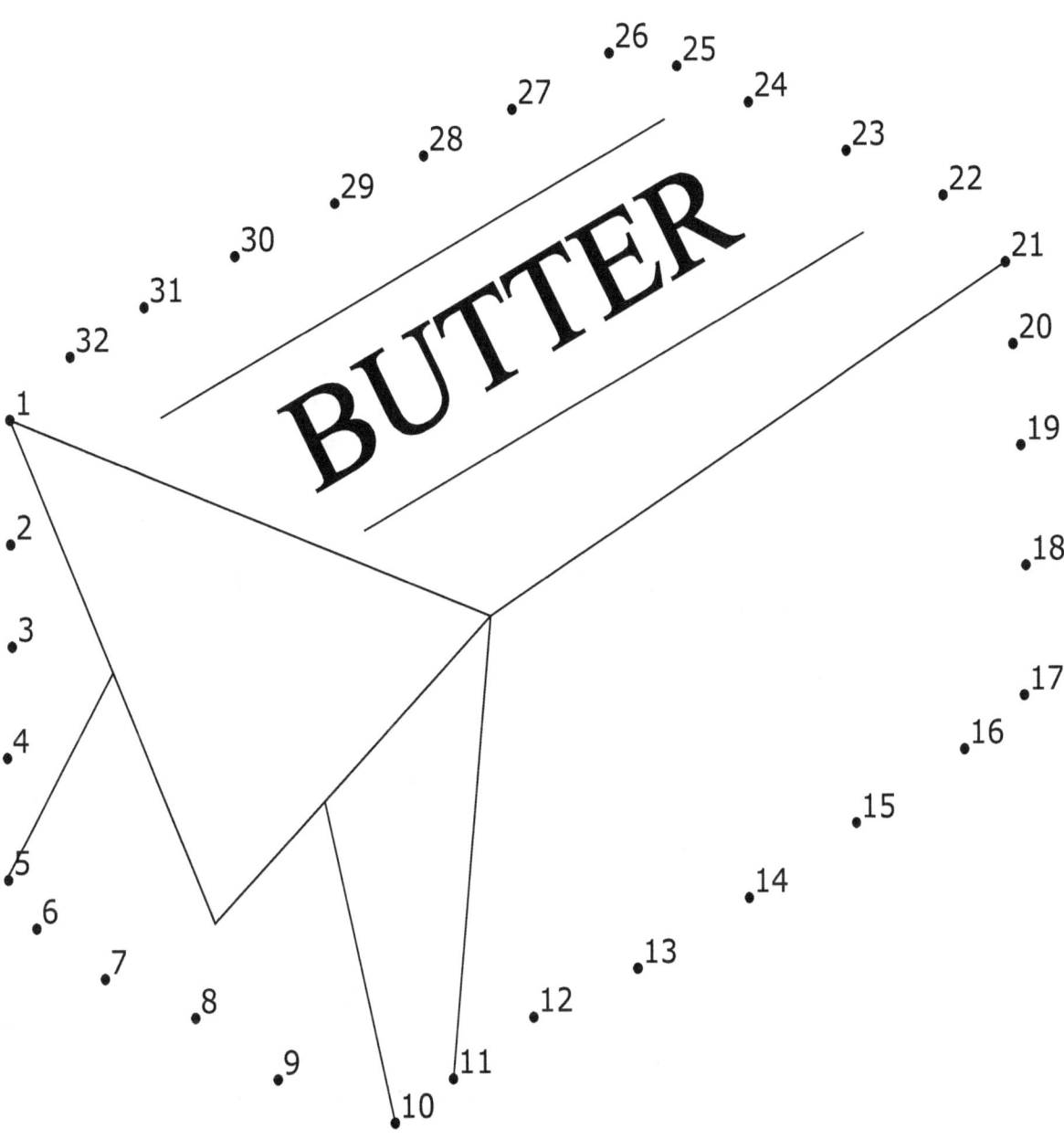

Cake

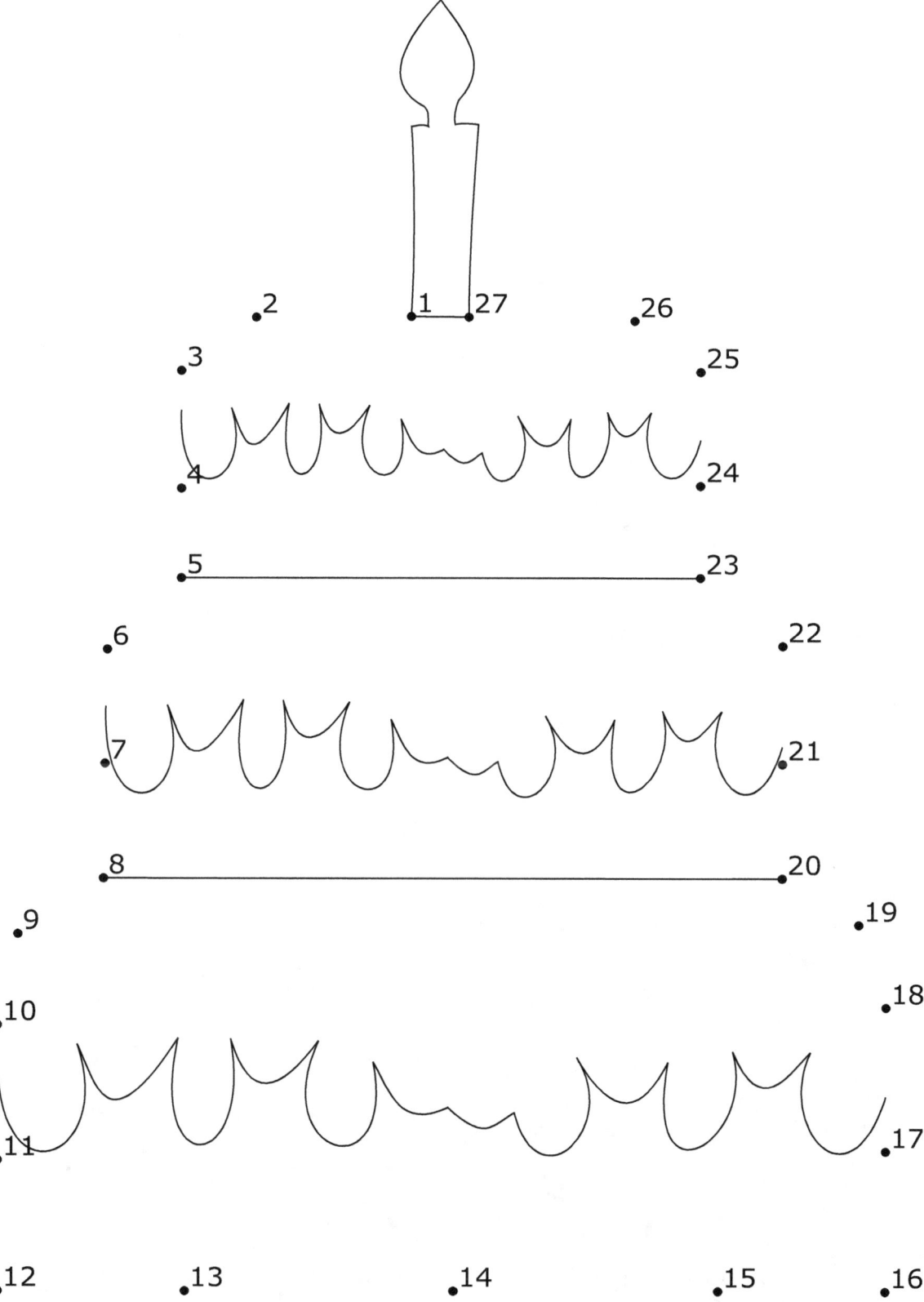

Carrot

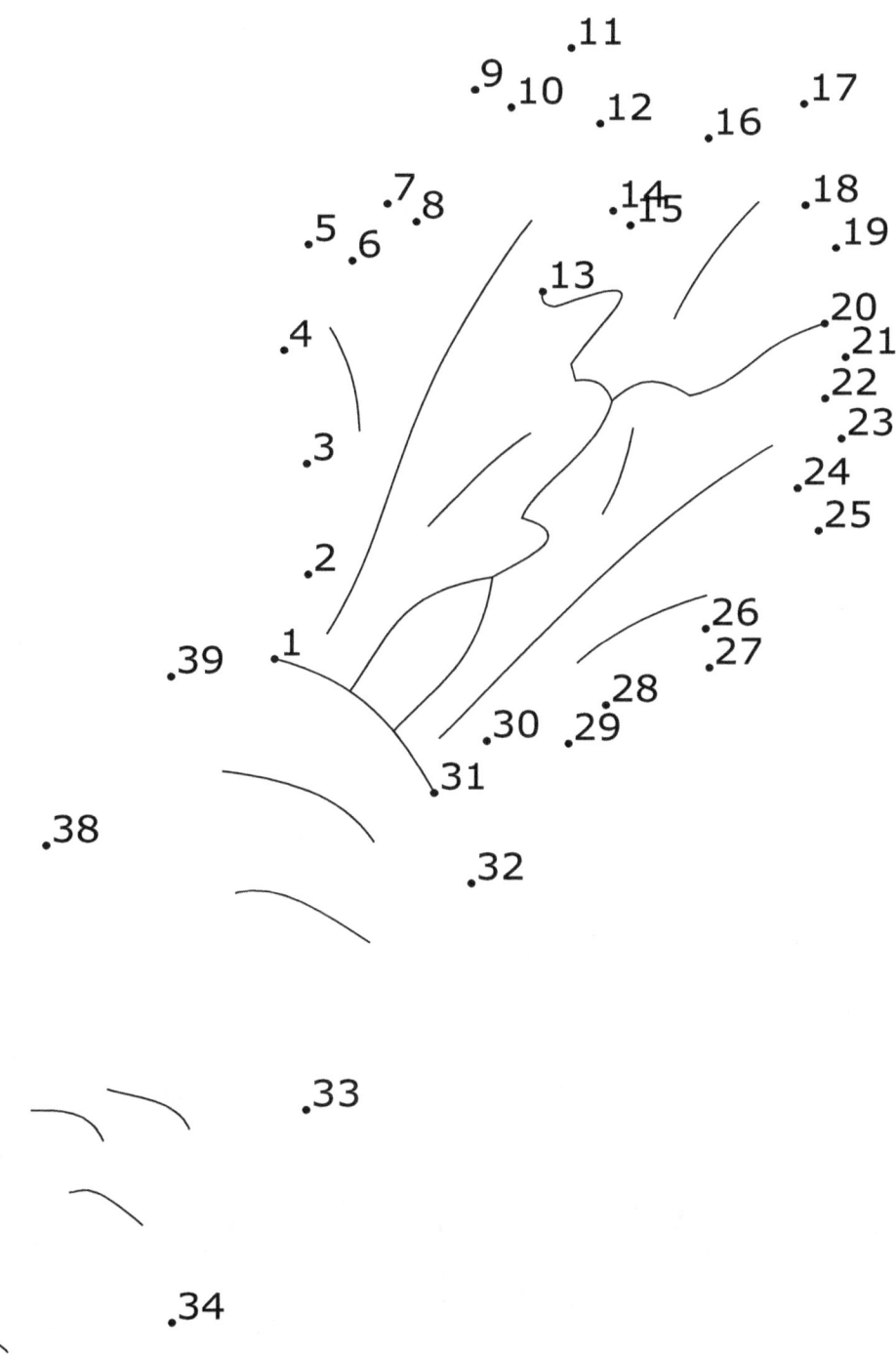

Carrot

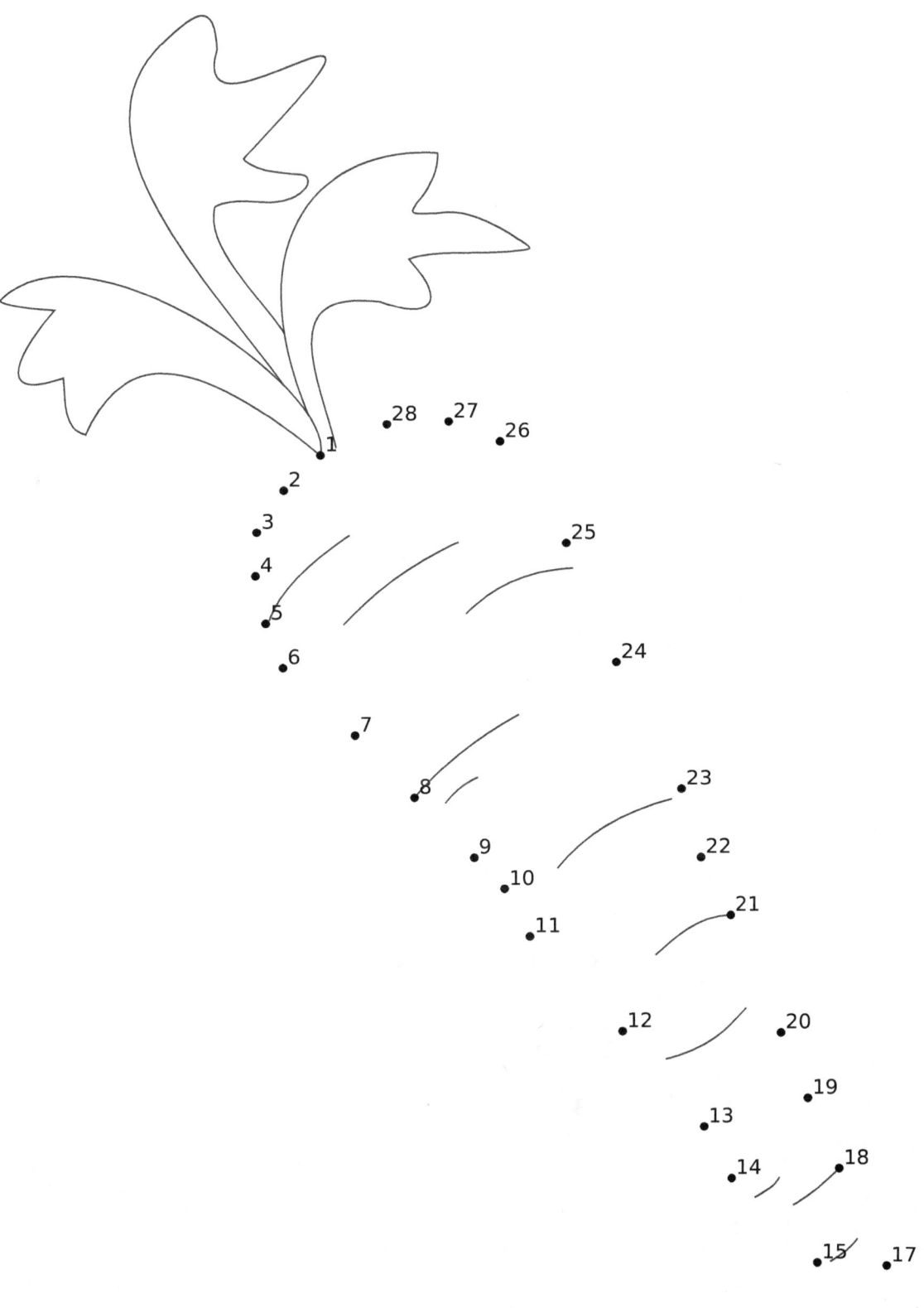

Cart

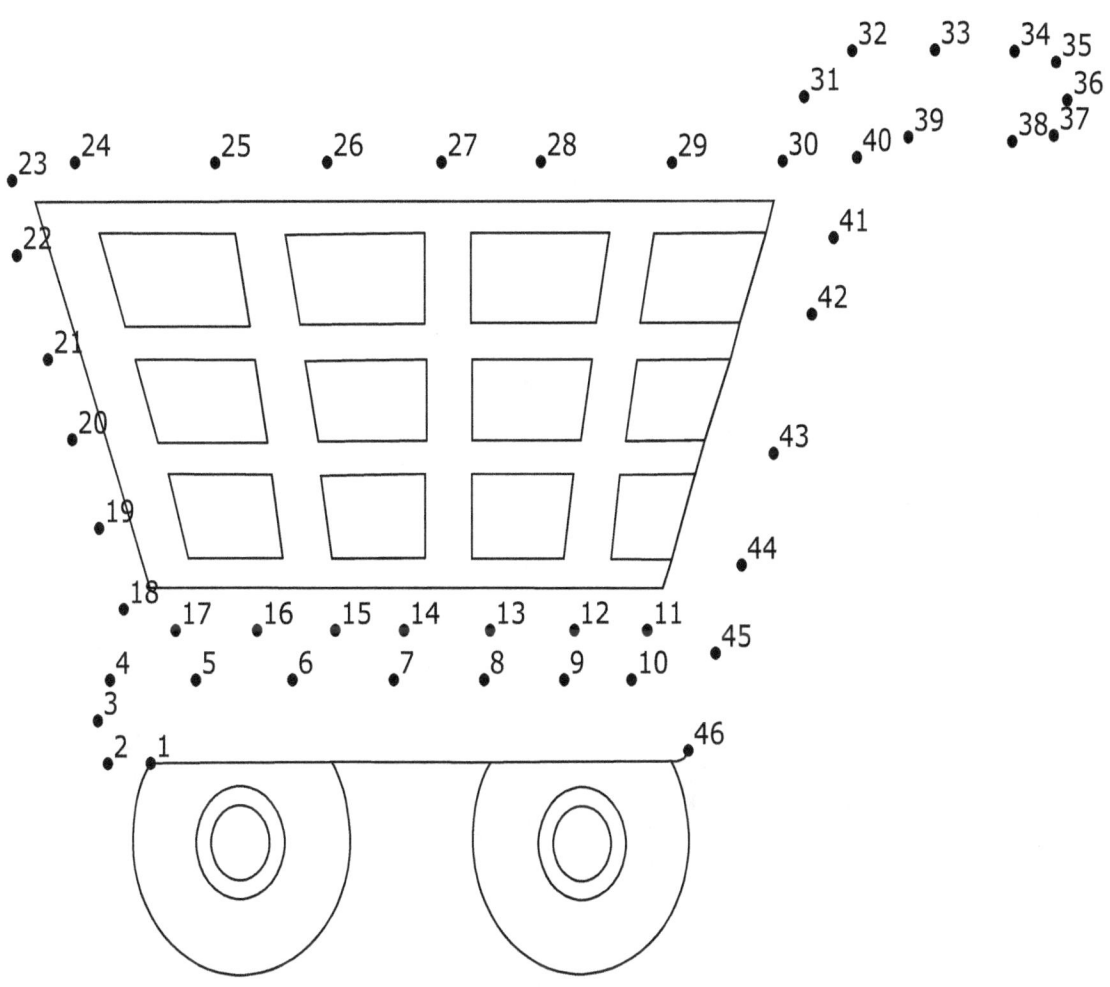

Cashier

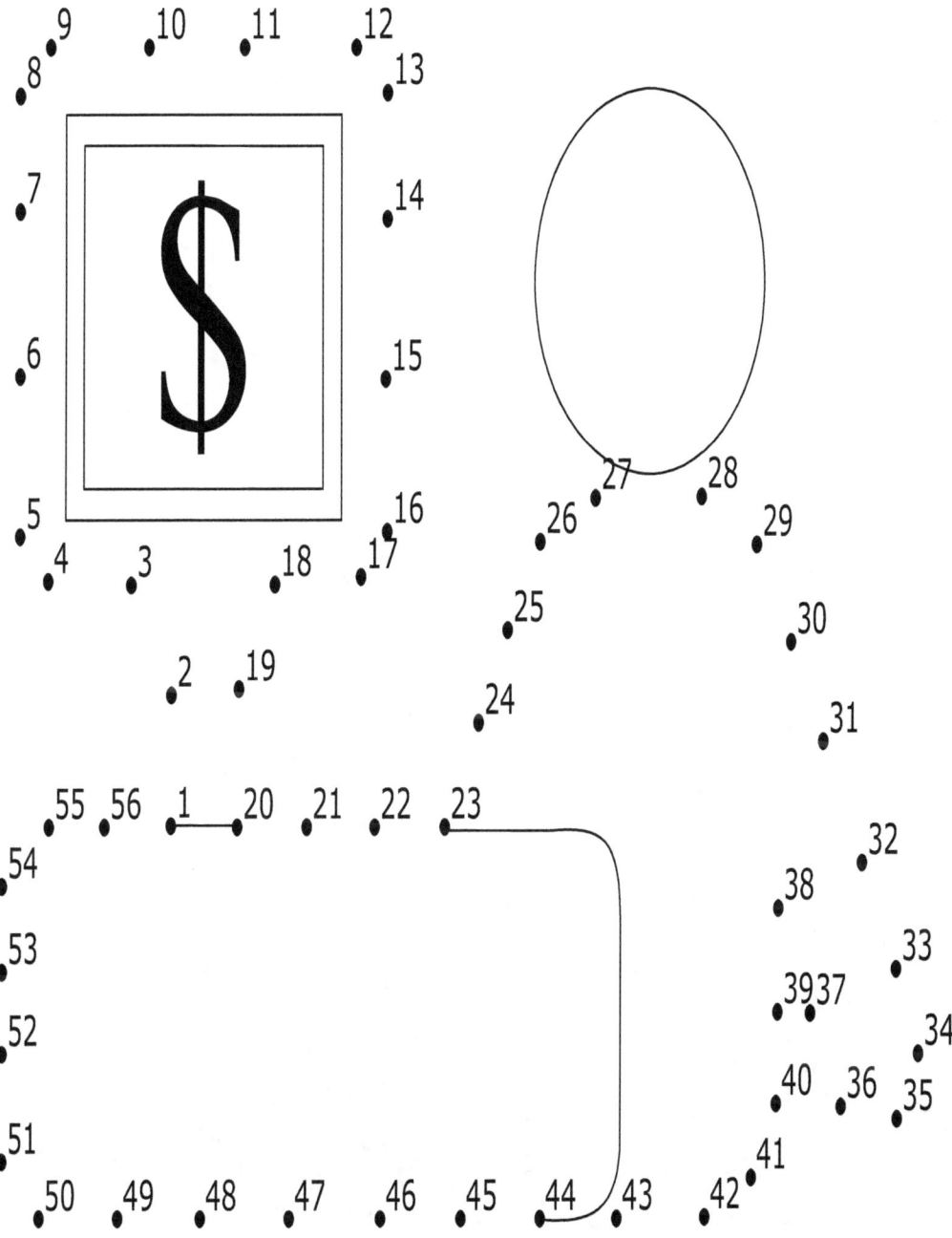

Celery

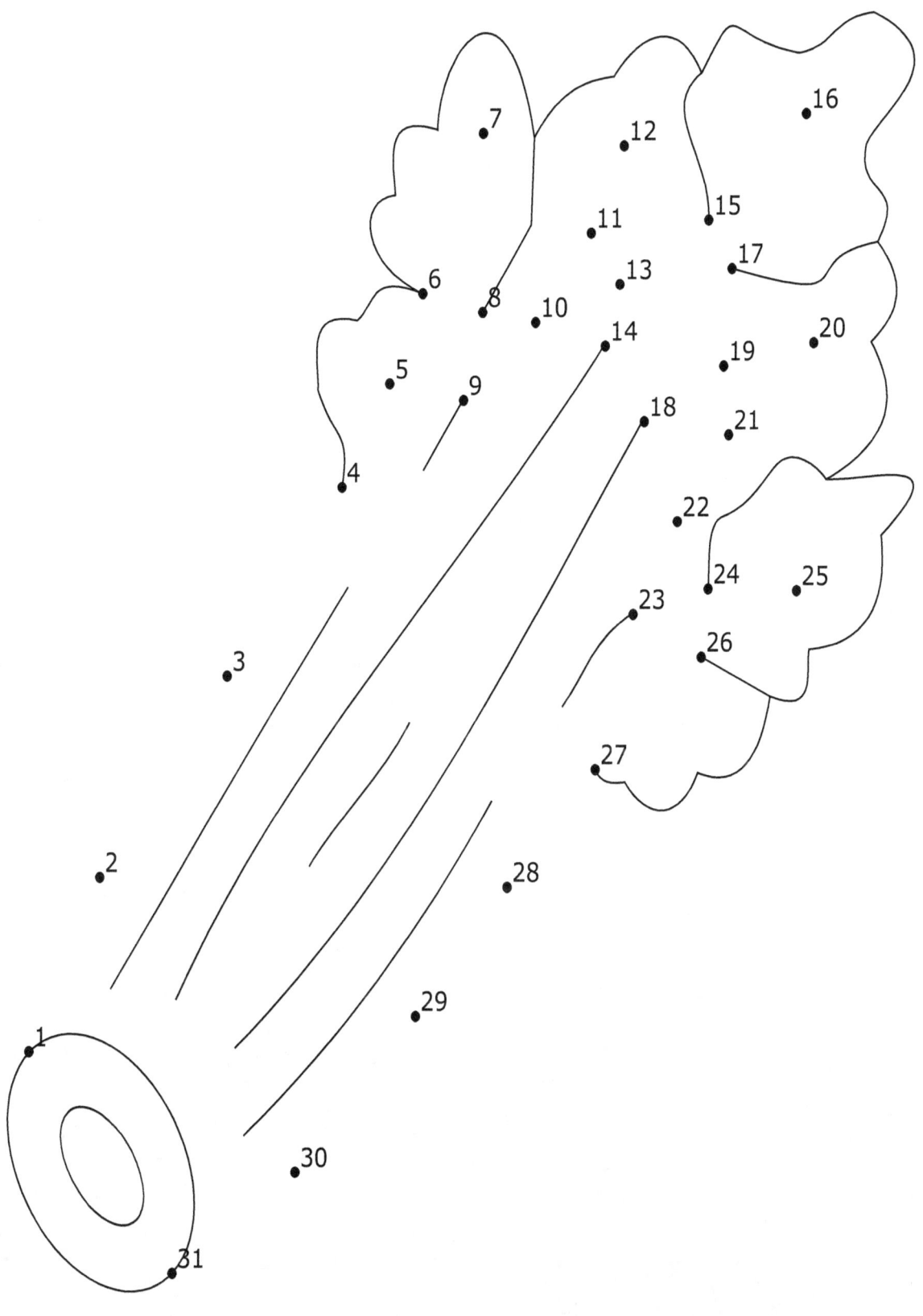

Cereal

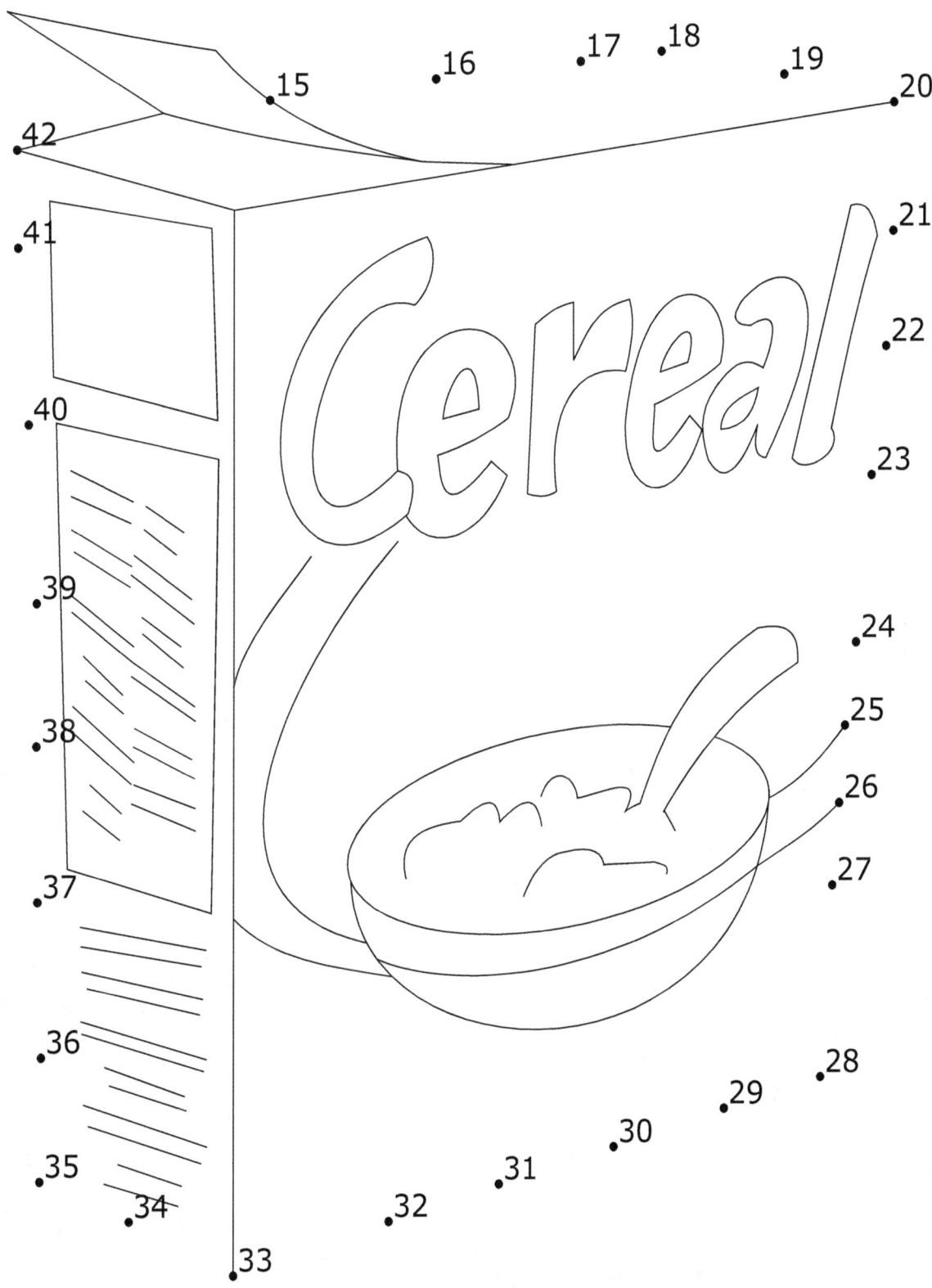

Cereal

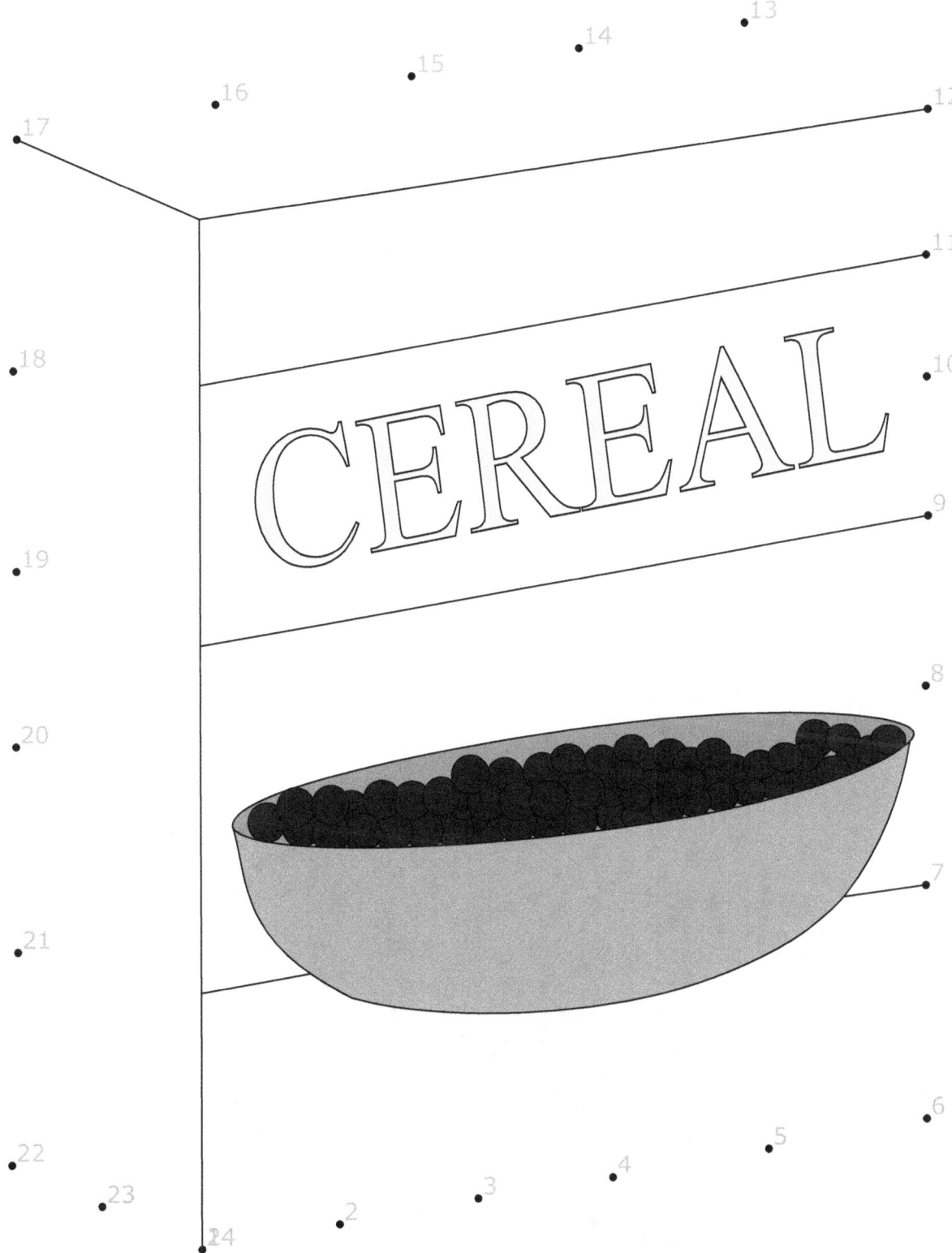

Champagne Bottle

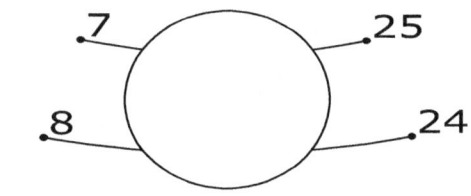

Check-Out

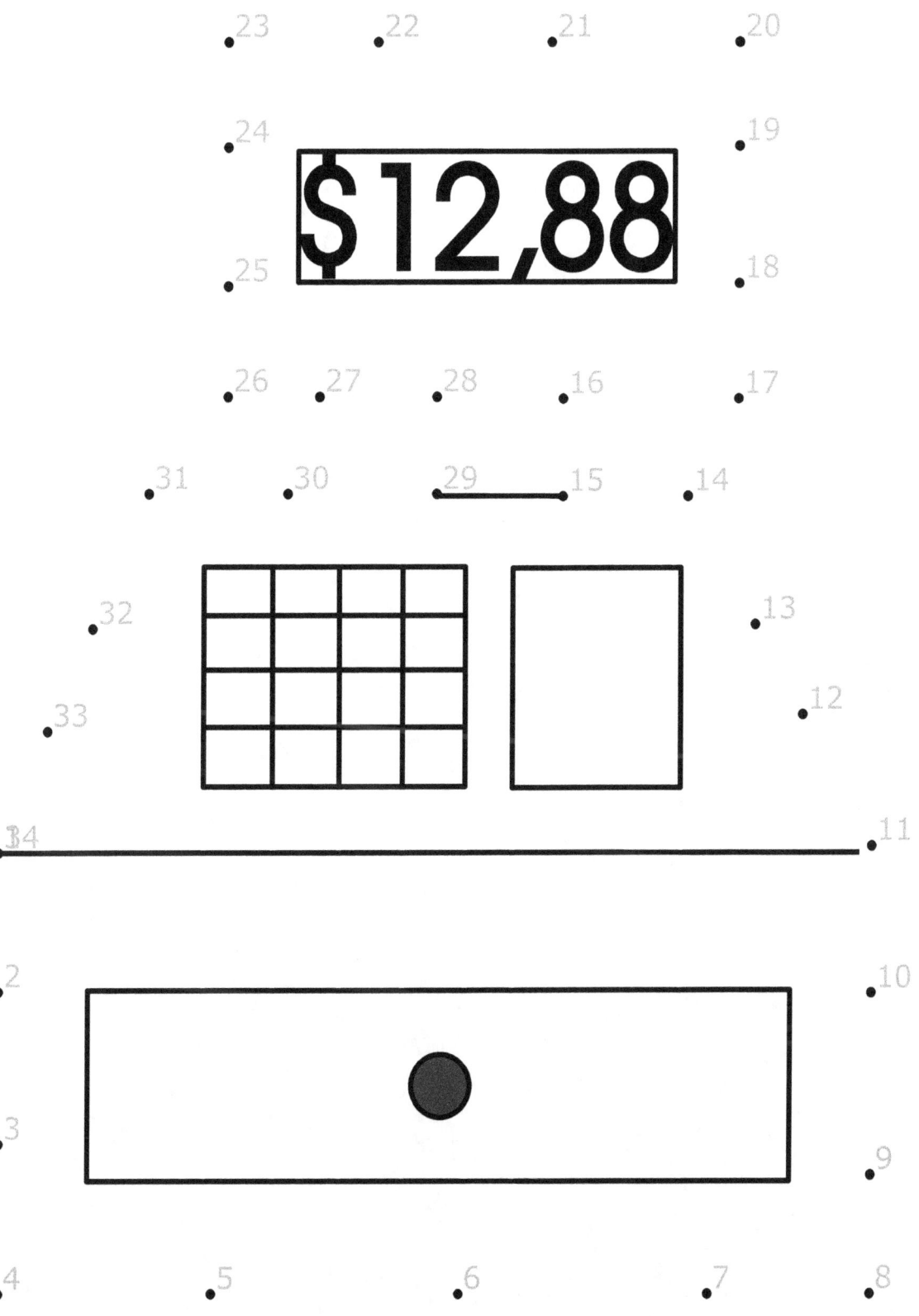

Cheese

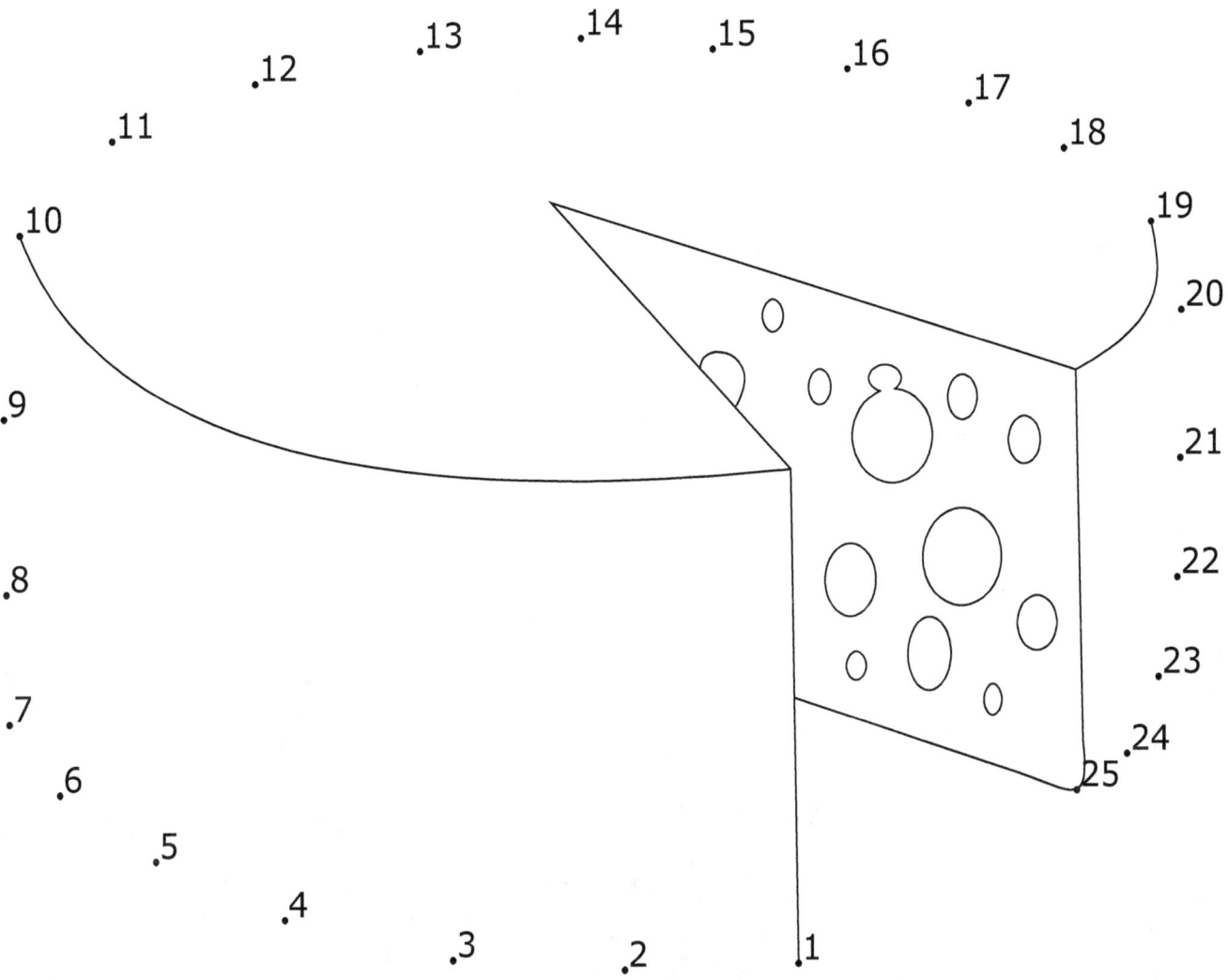

Cheese

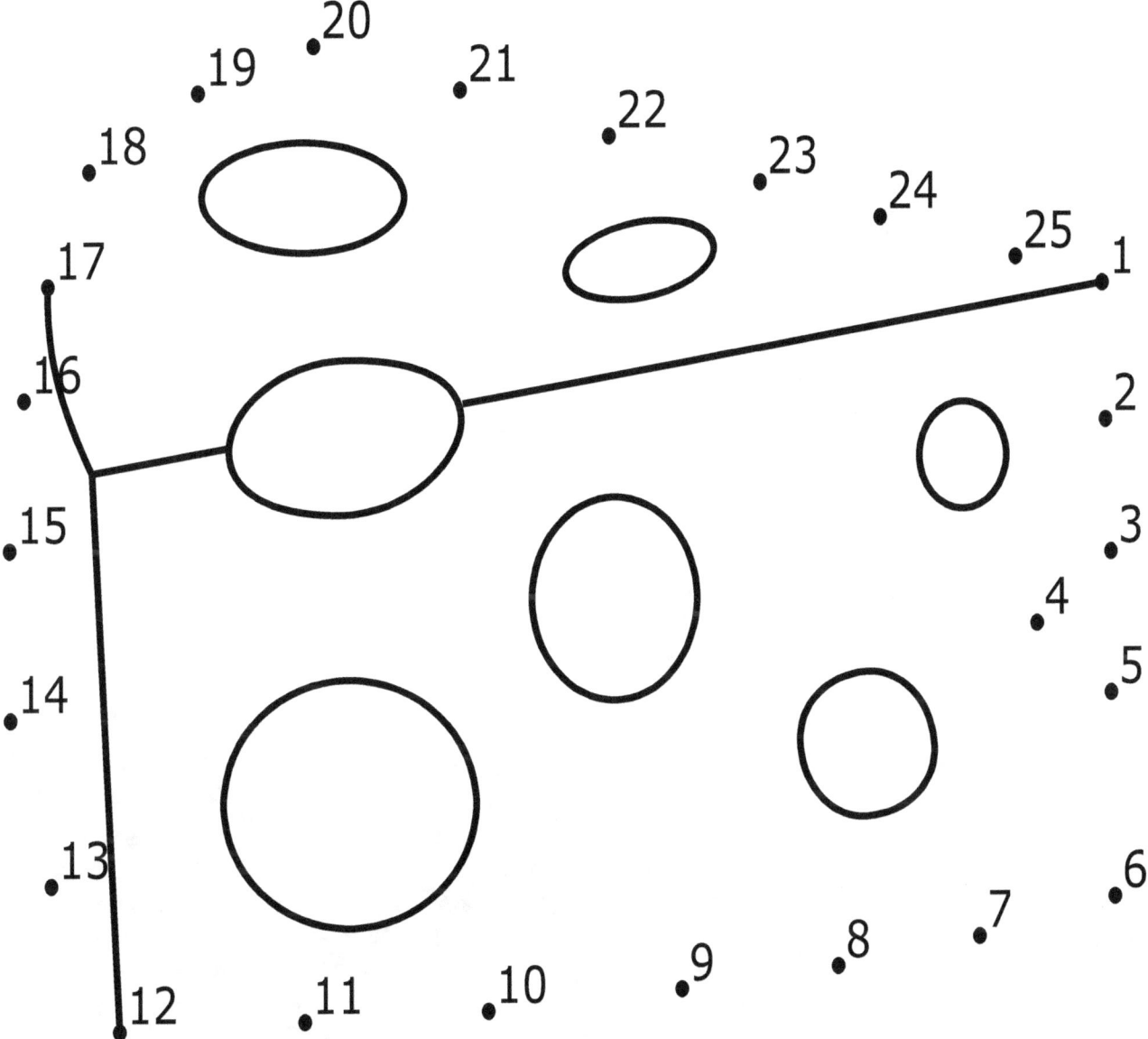

Chewing Gum

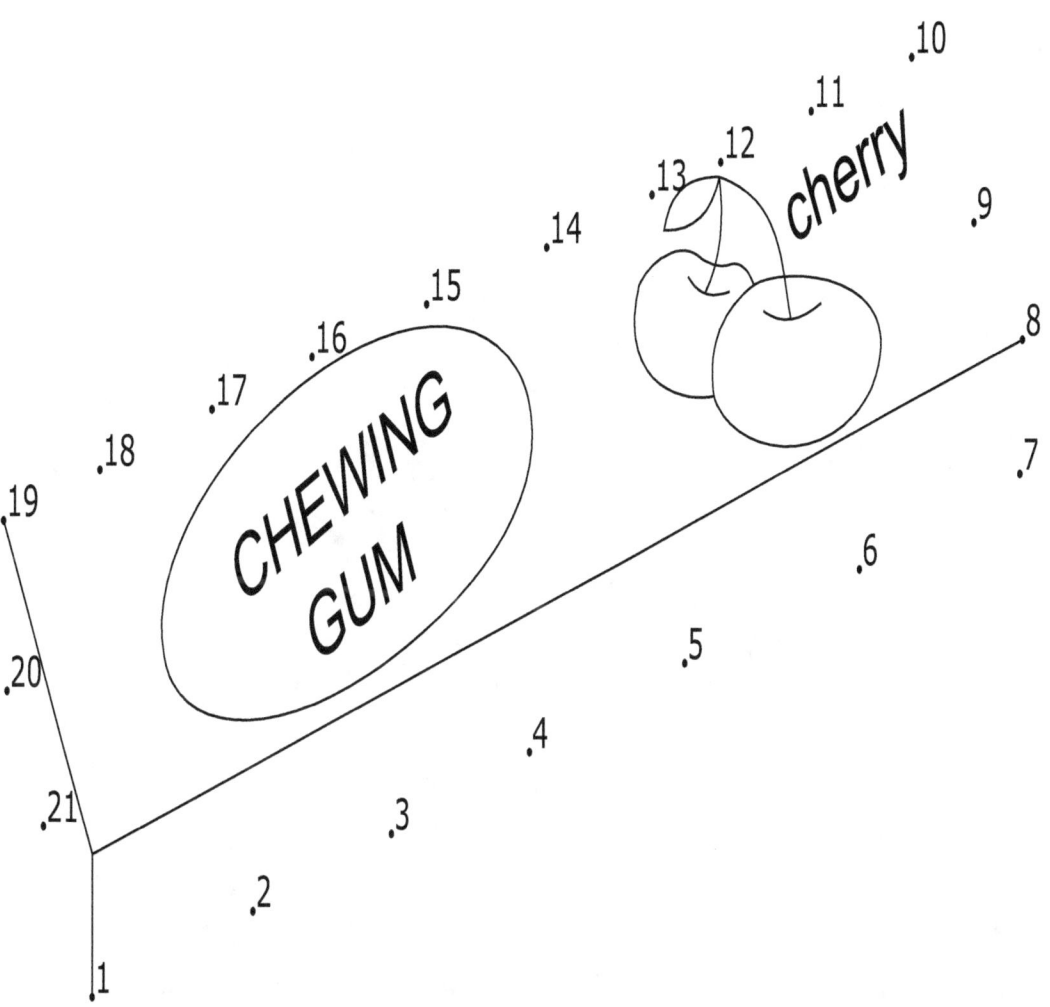

Chicken

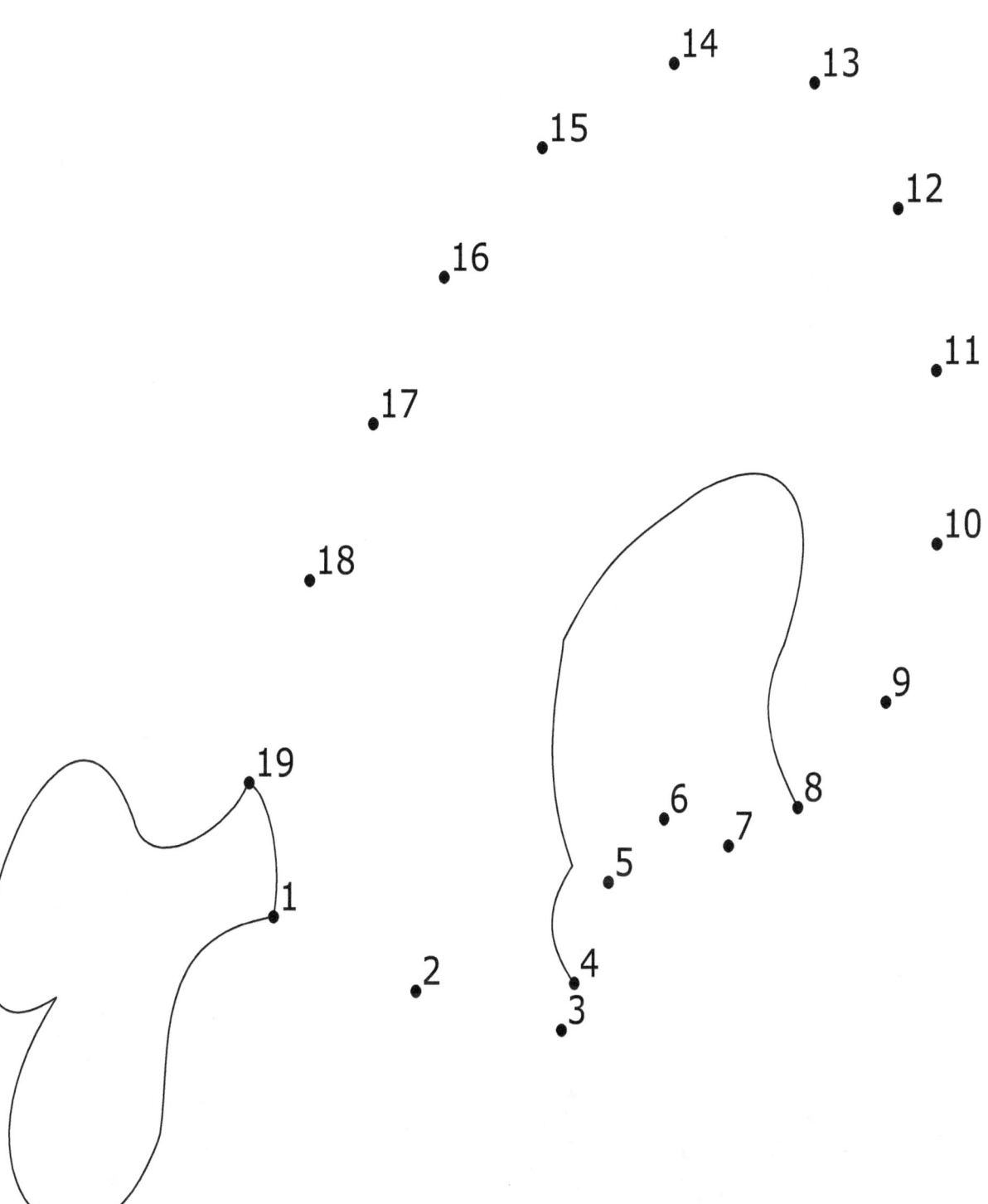

Citrus Fruit

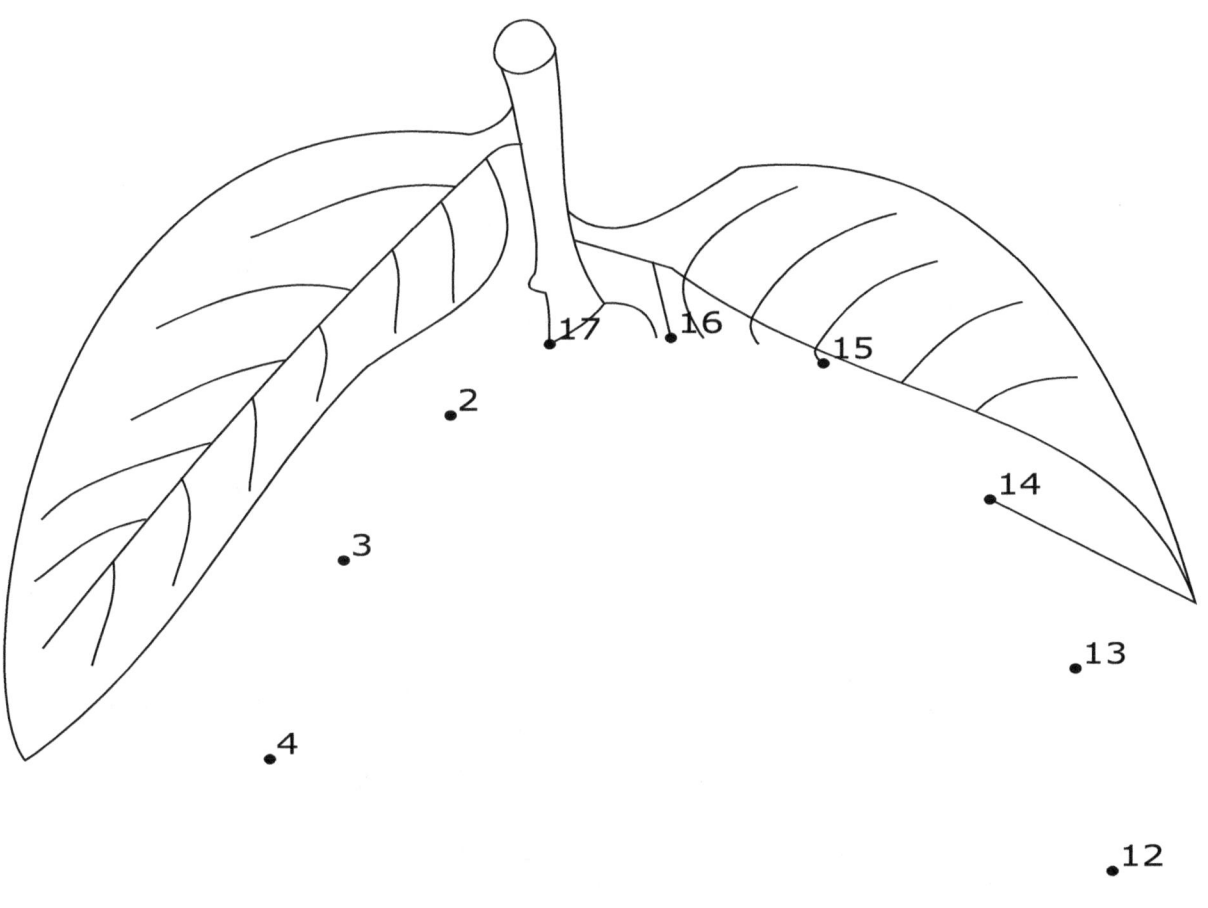

Dishwasher Liquid

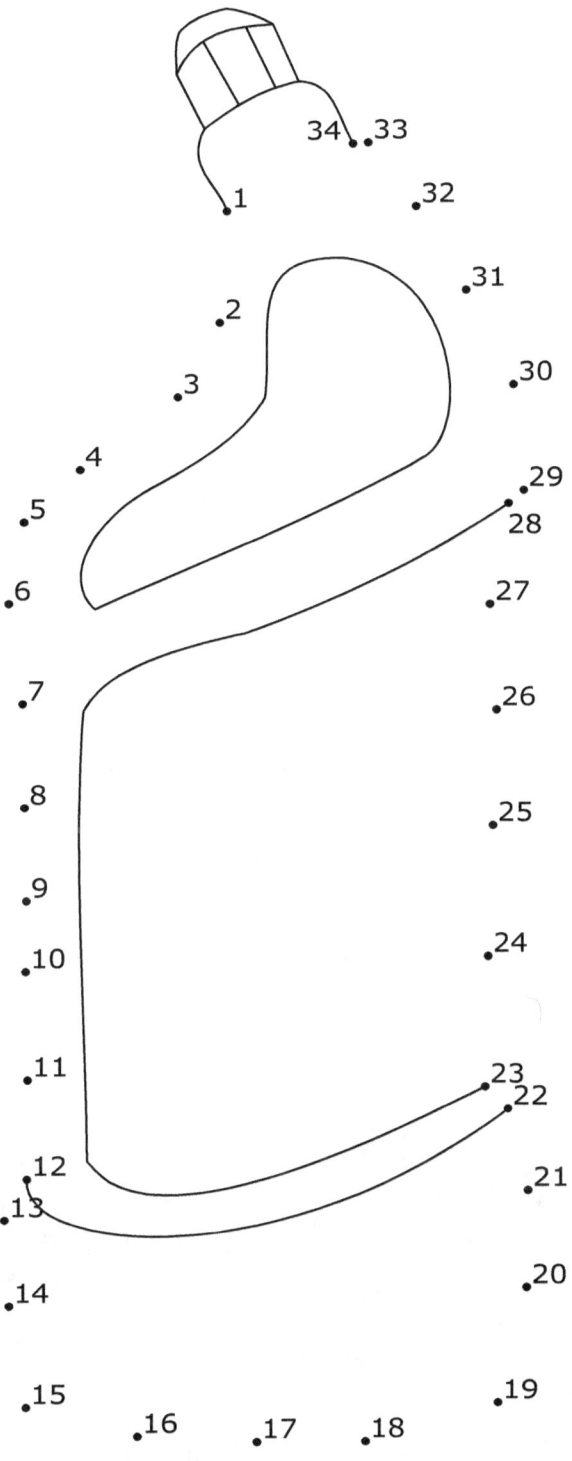

Disinfectant

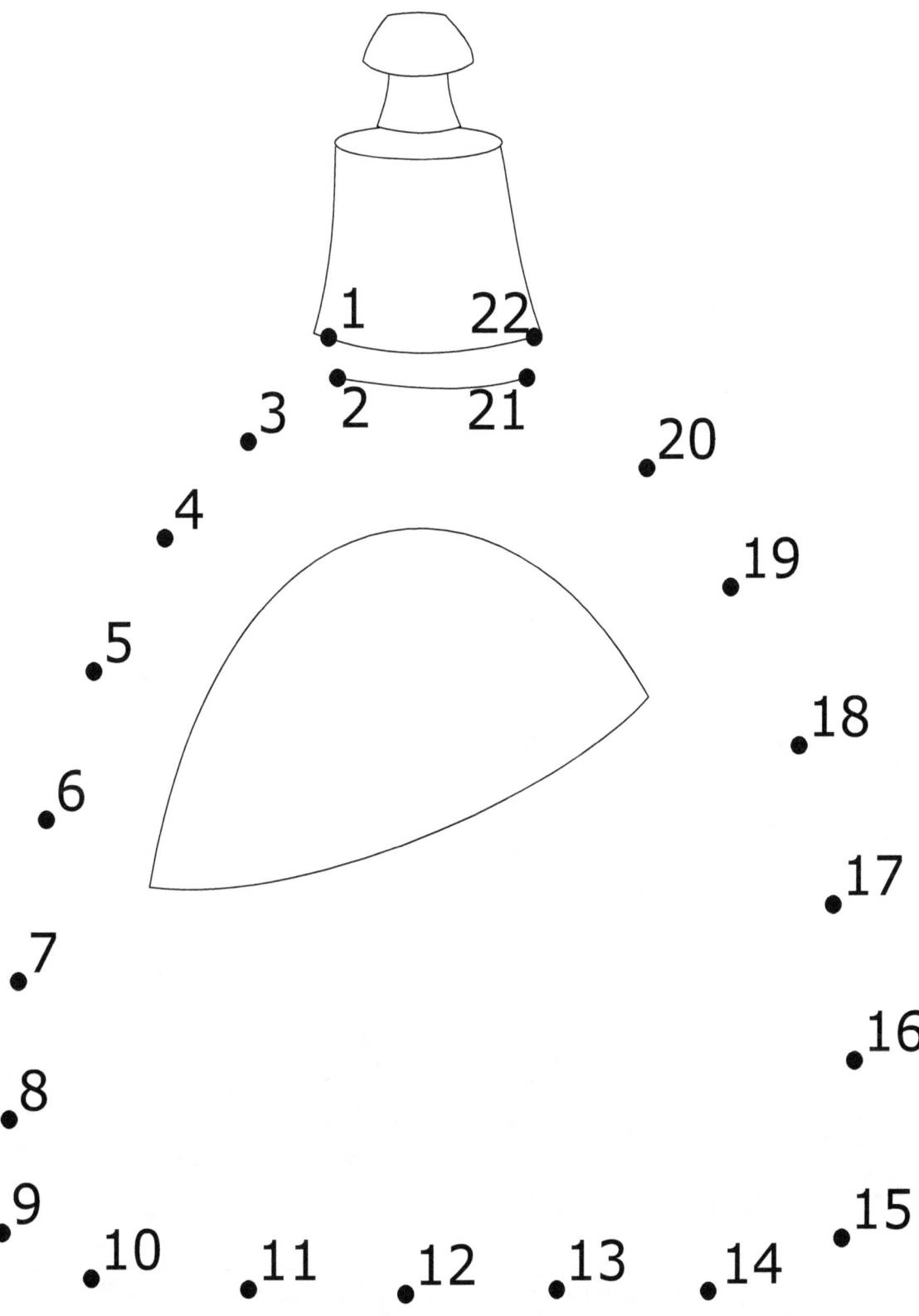

Dog Food

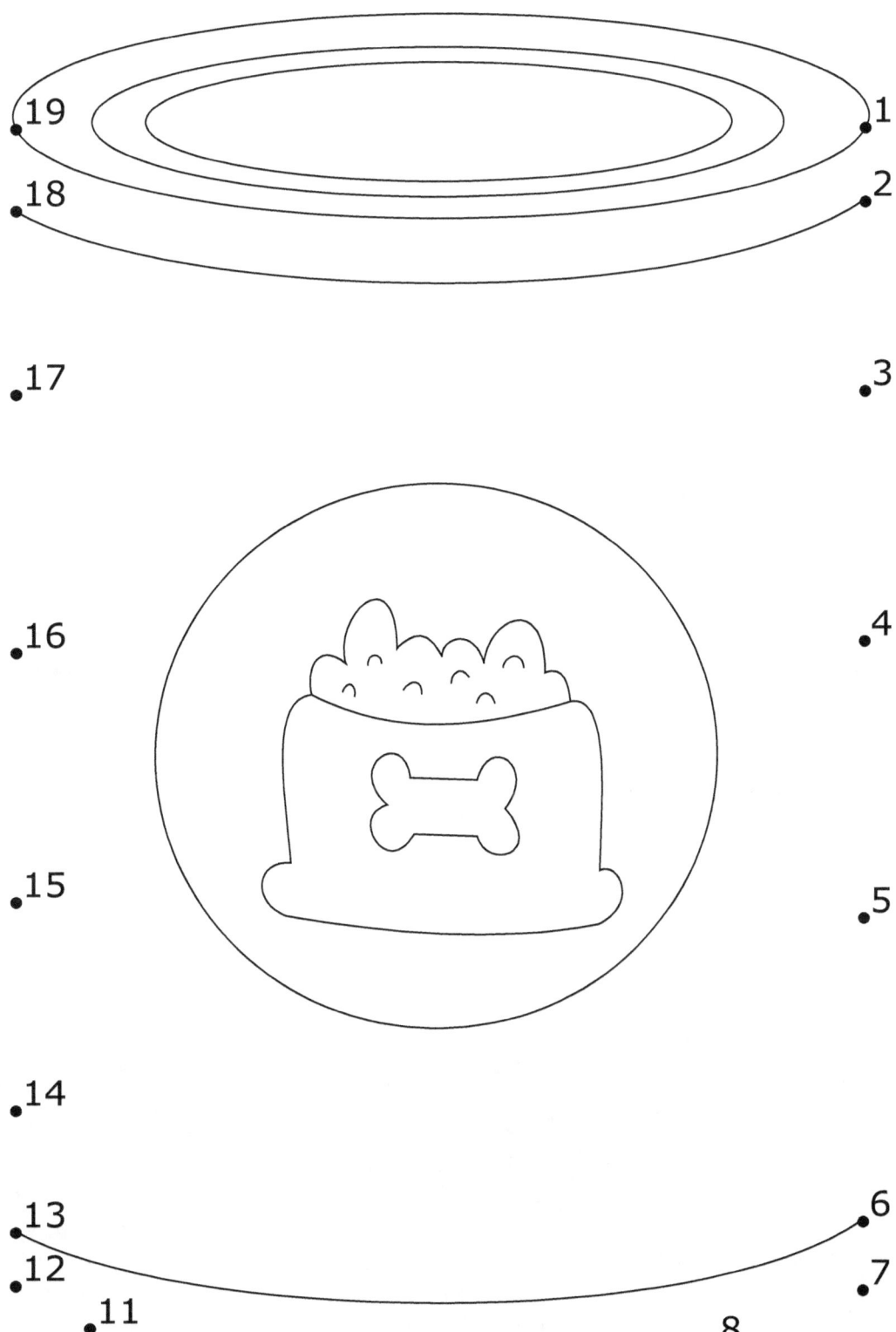

Eggs

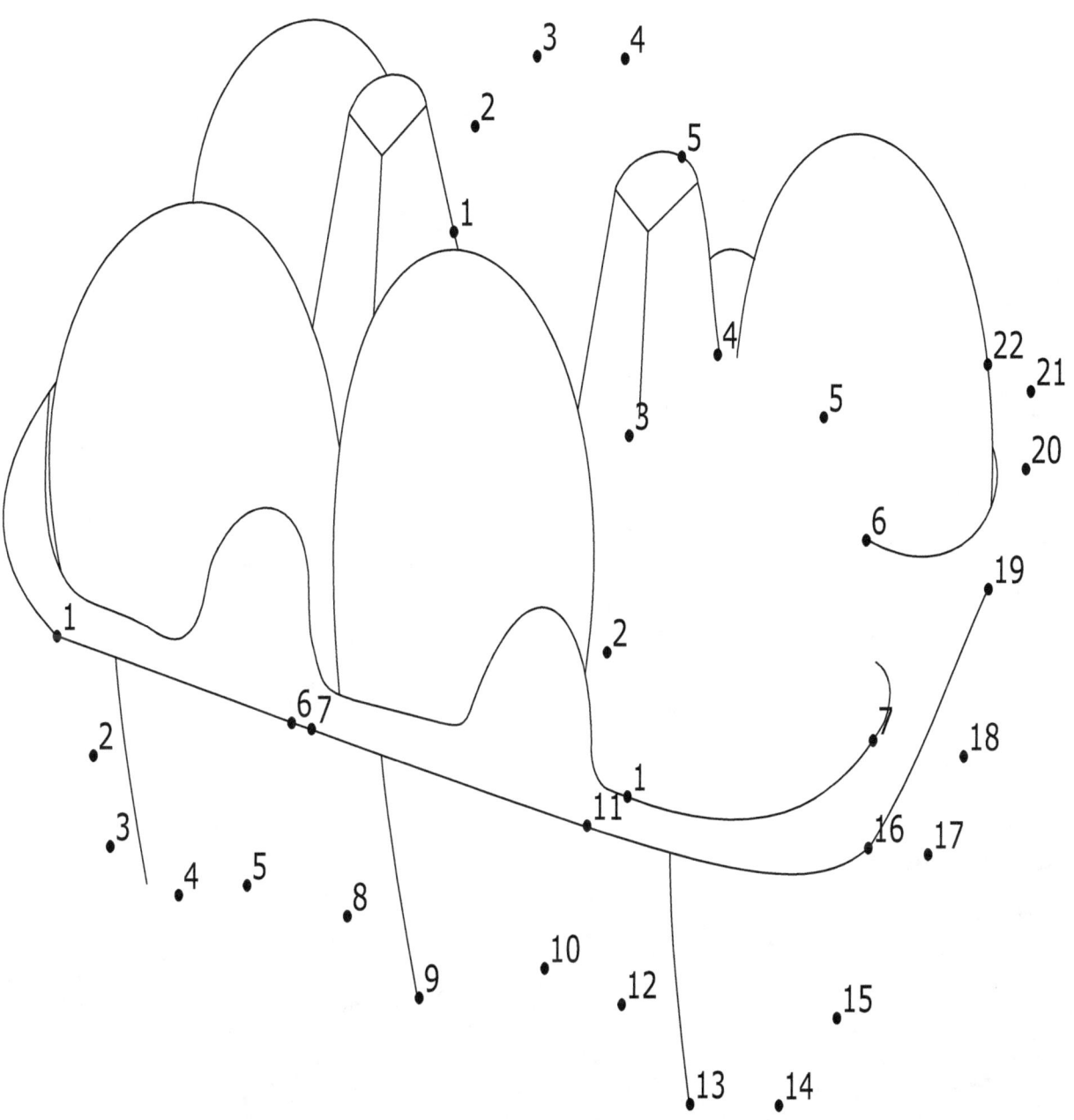

Fish

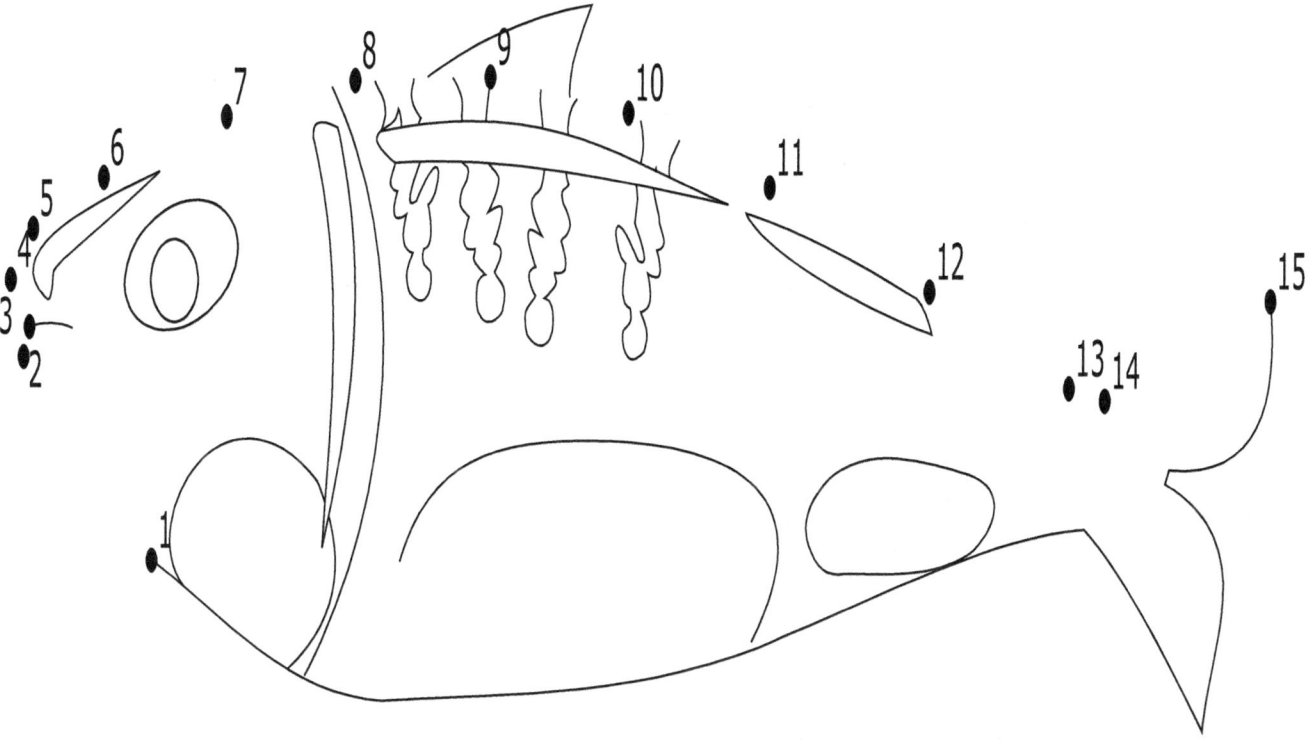

Flour

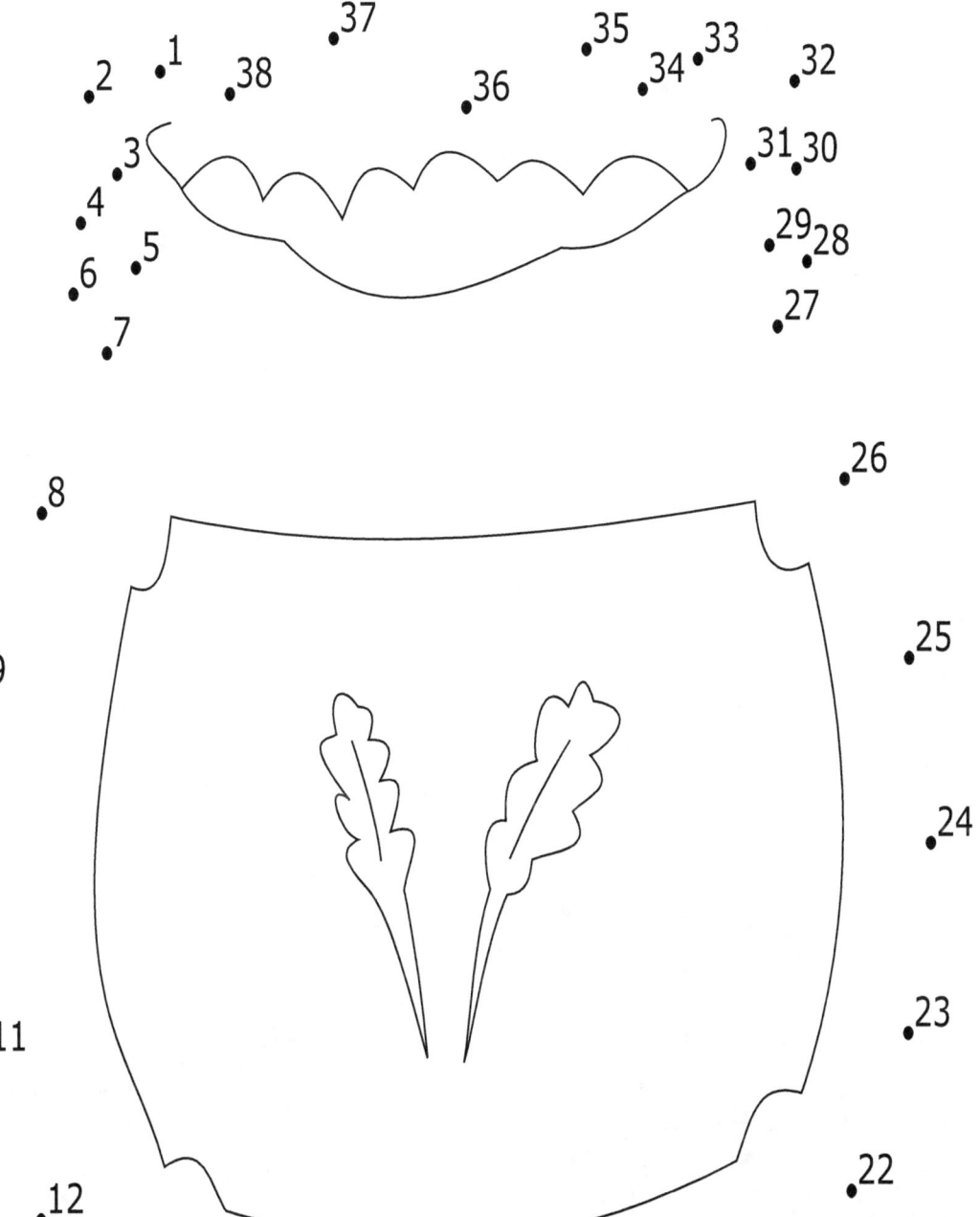

Fruit Juice

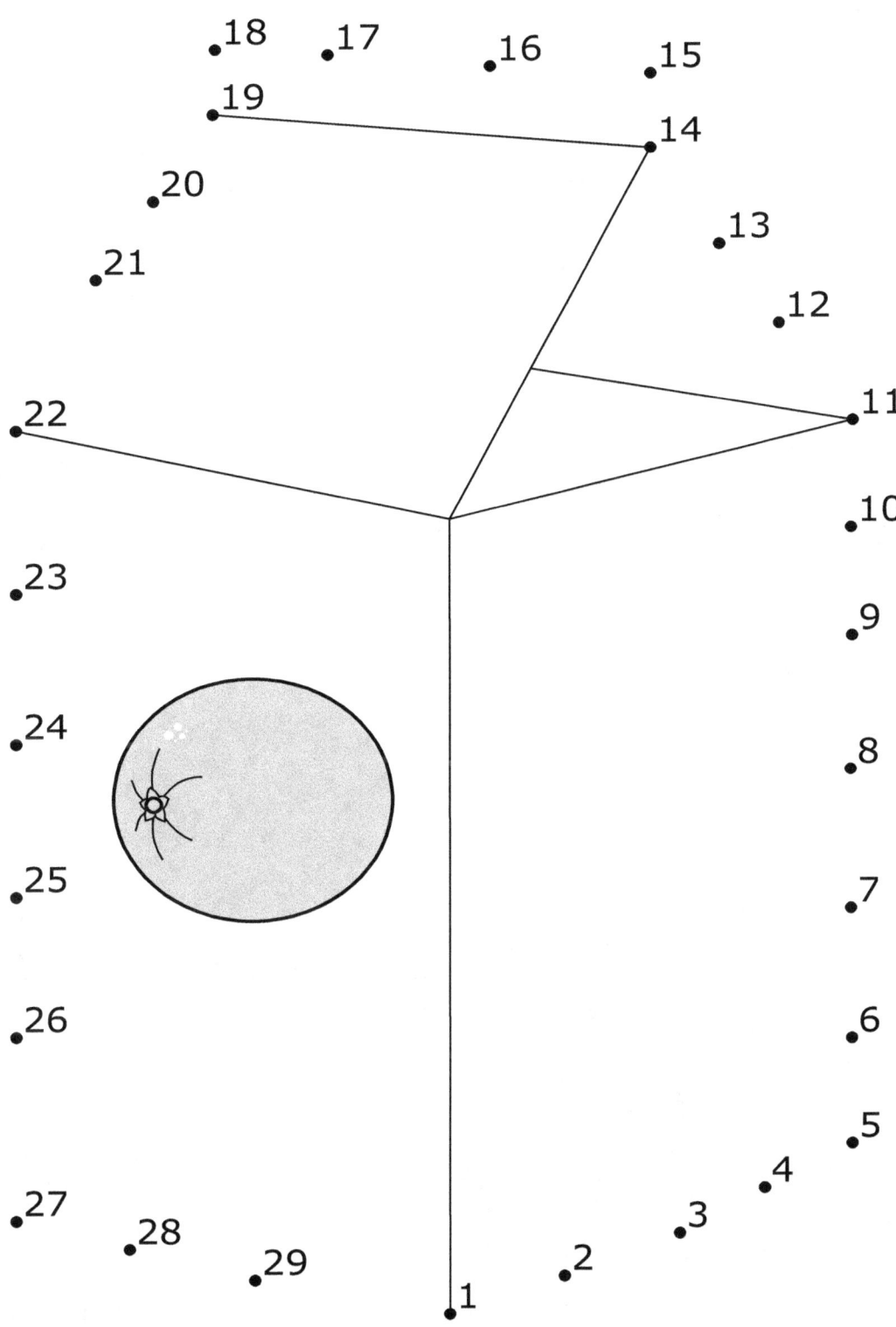

Glass Cleaner

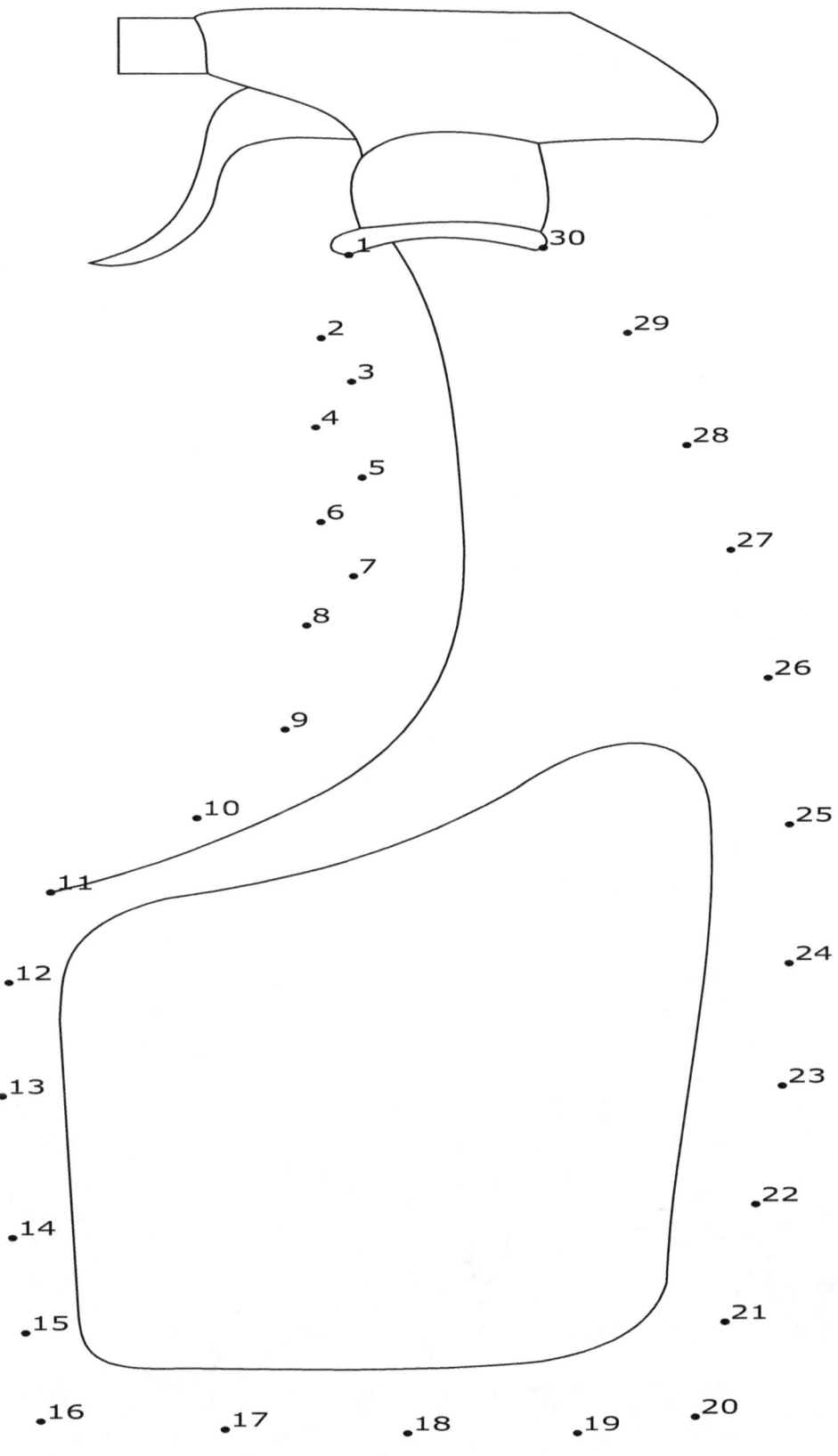

Grape

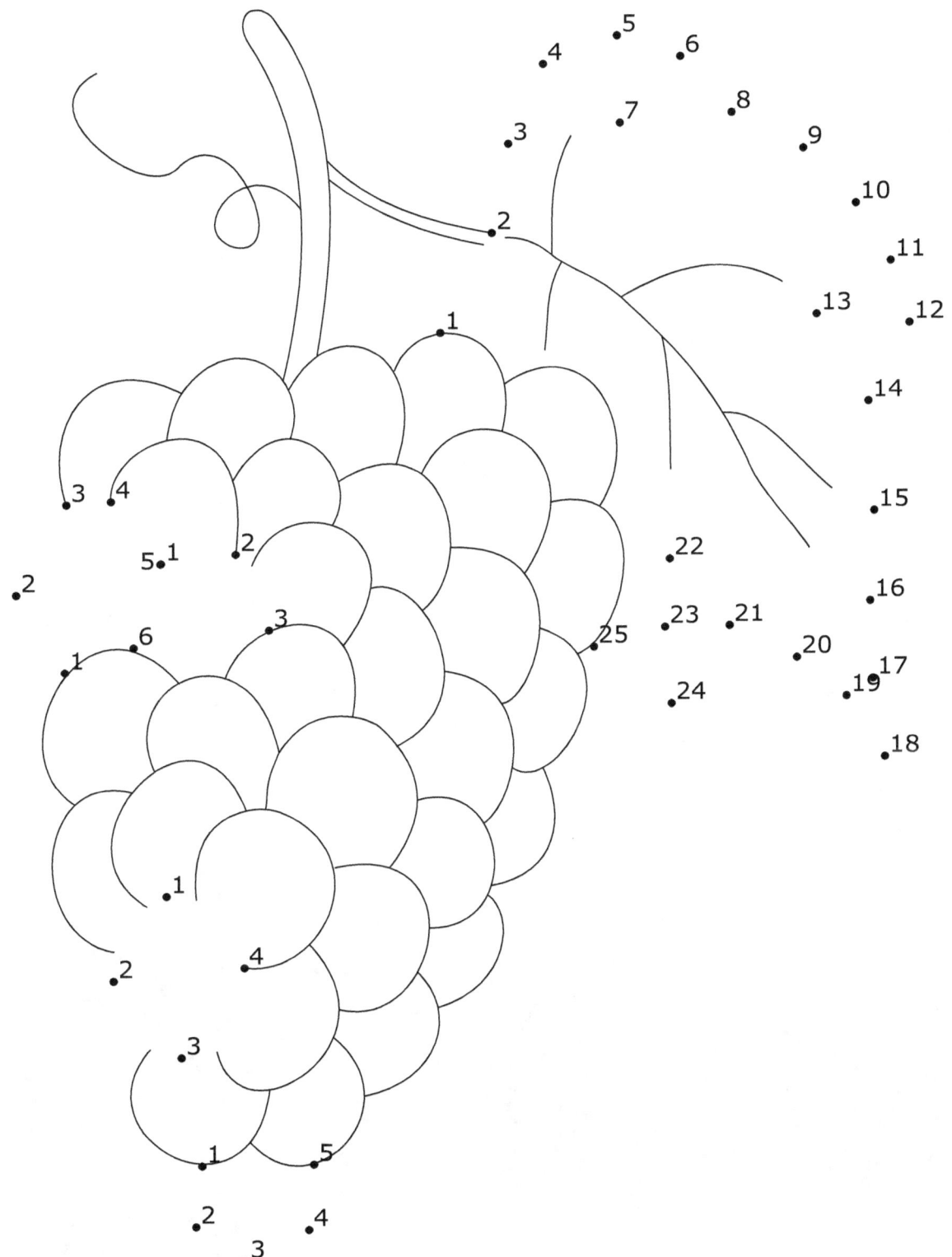

Ham

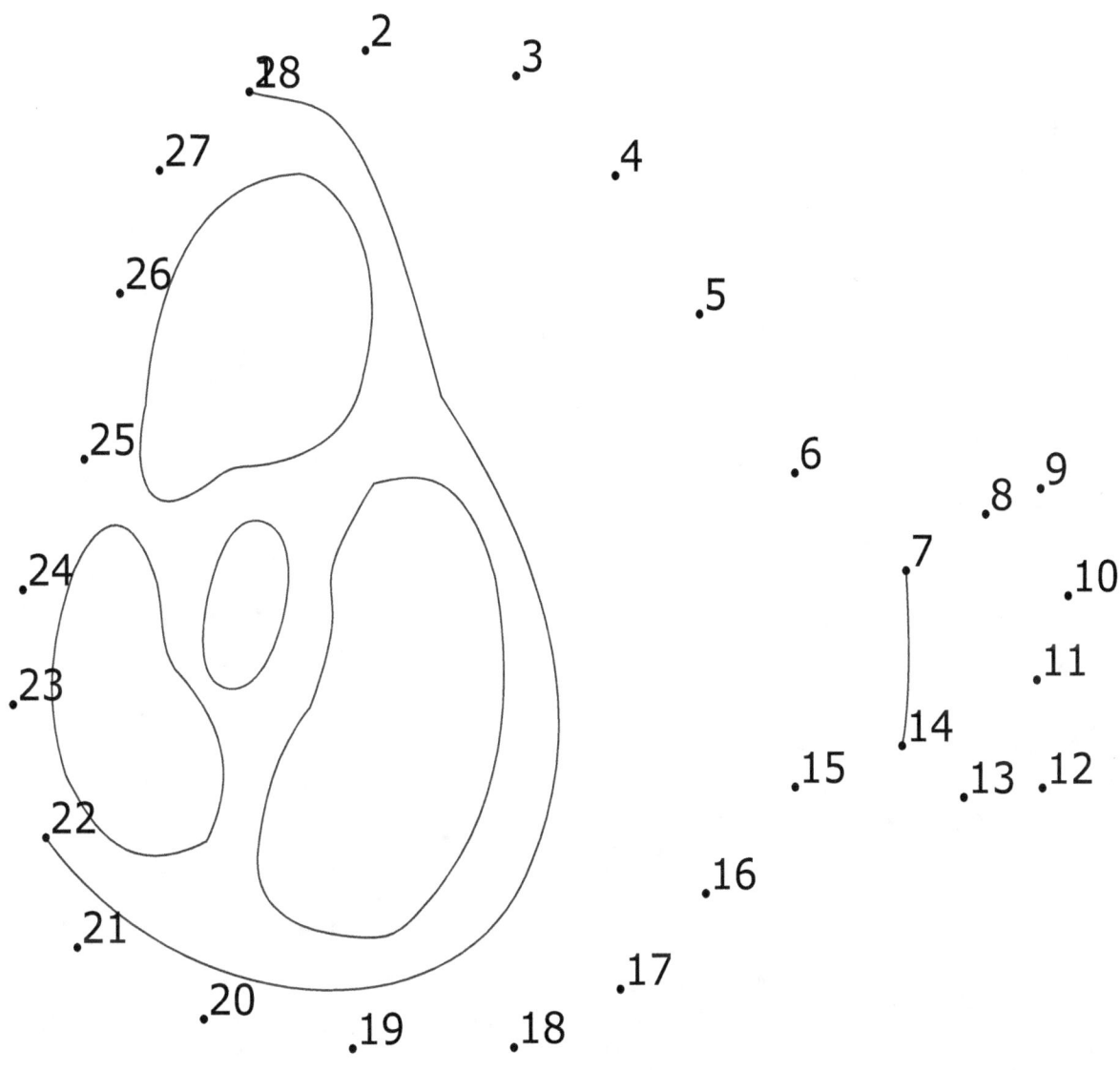

Hamburger

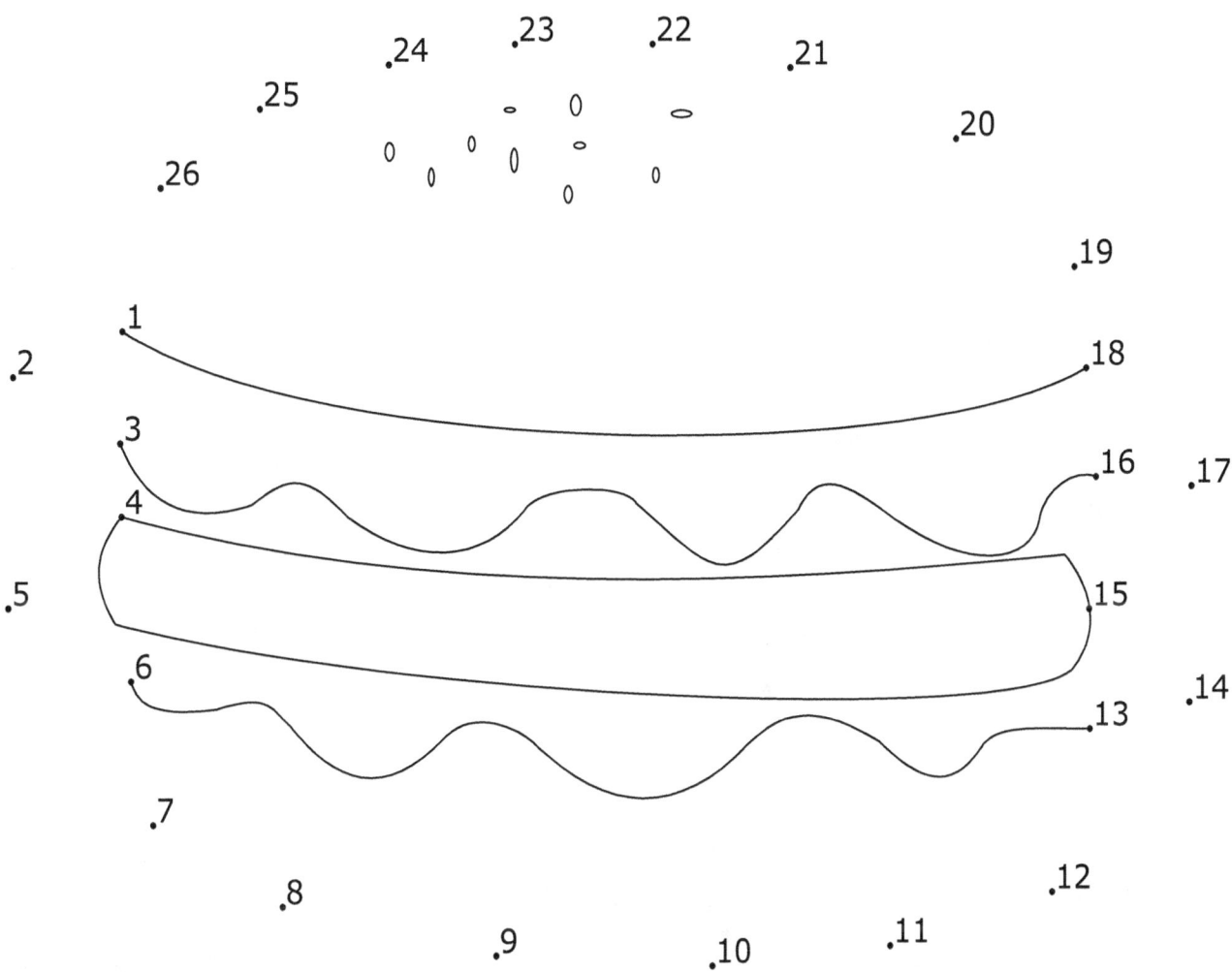

Hand Soap

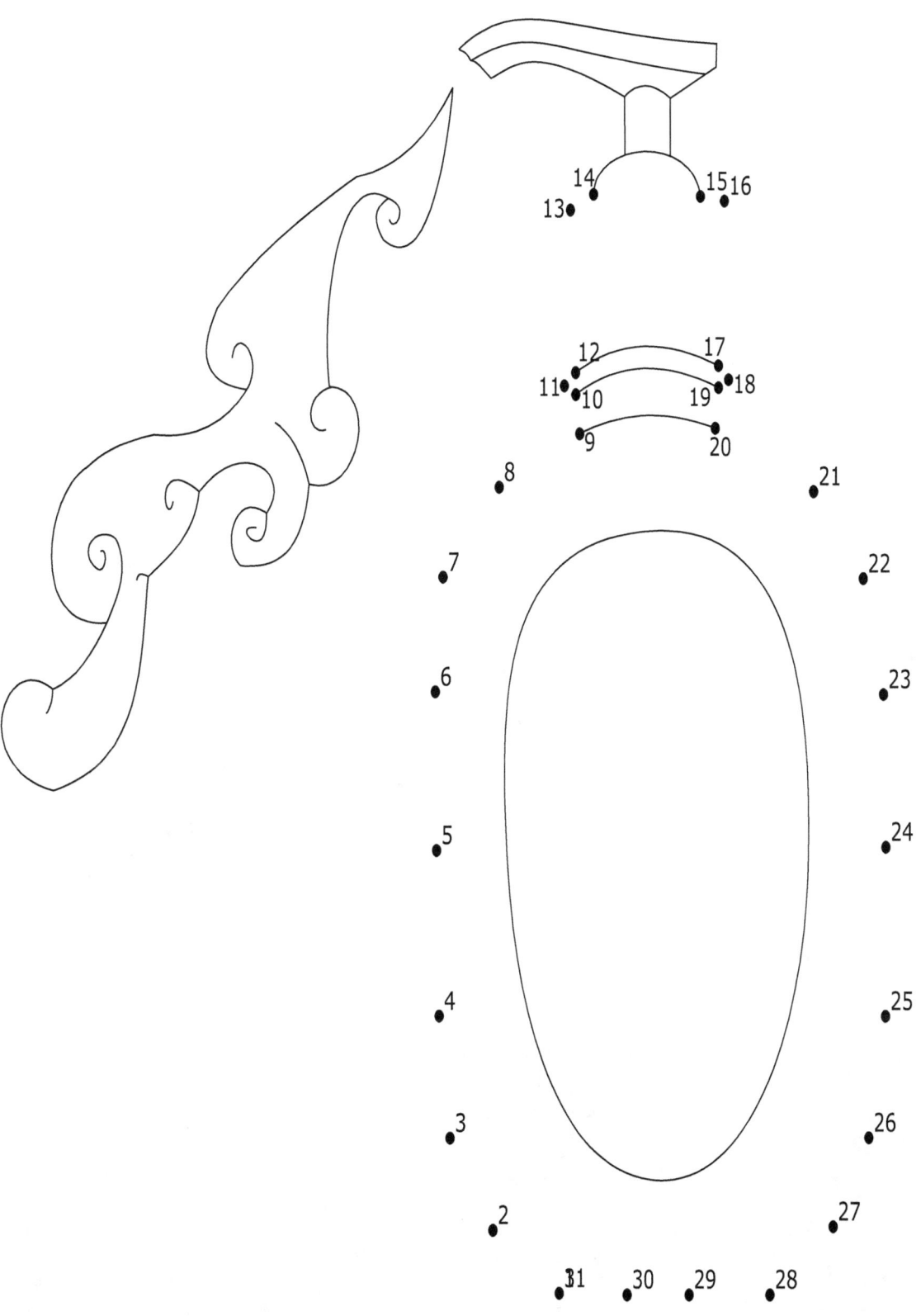

Ice Cream

Kitchen Roll

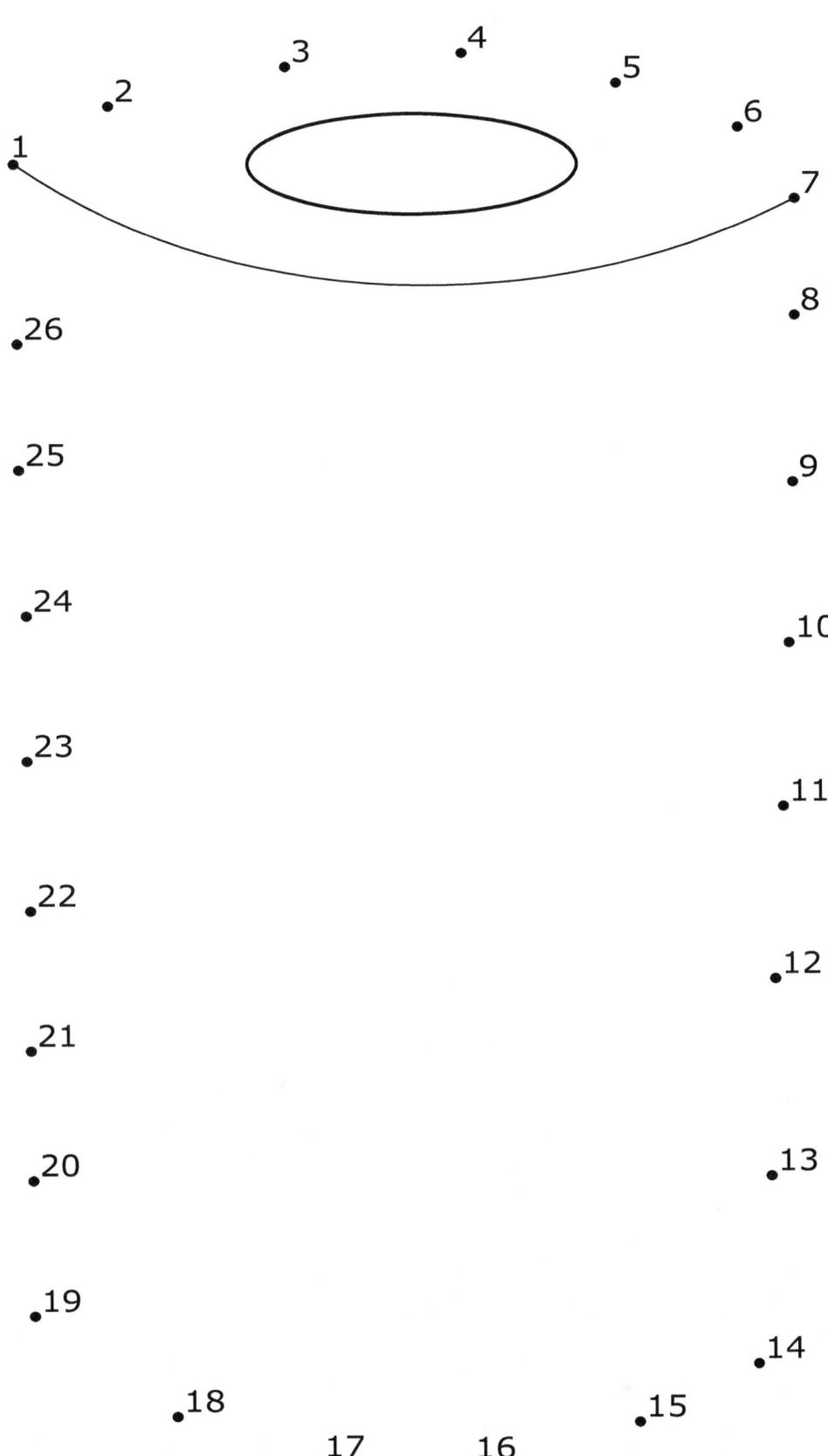

Lettuce

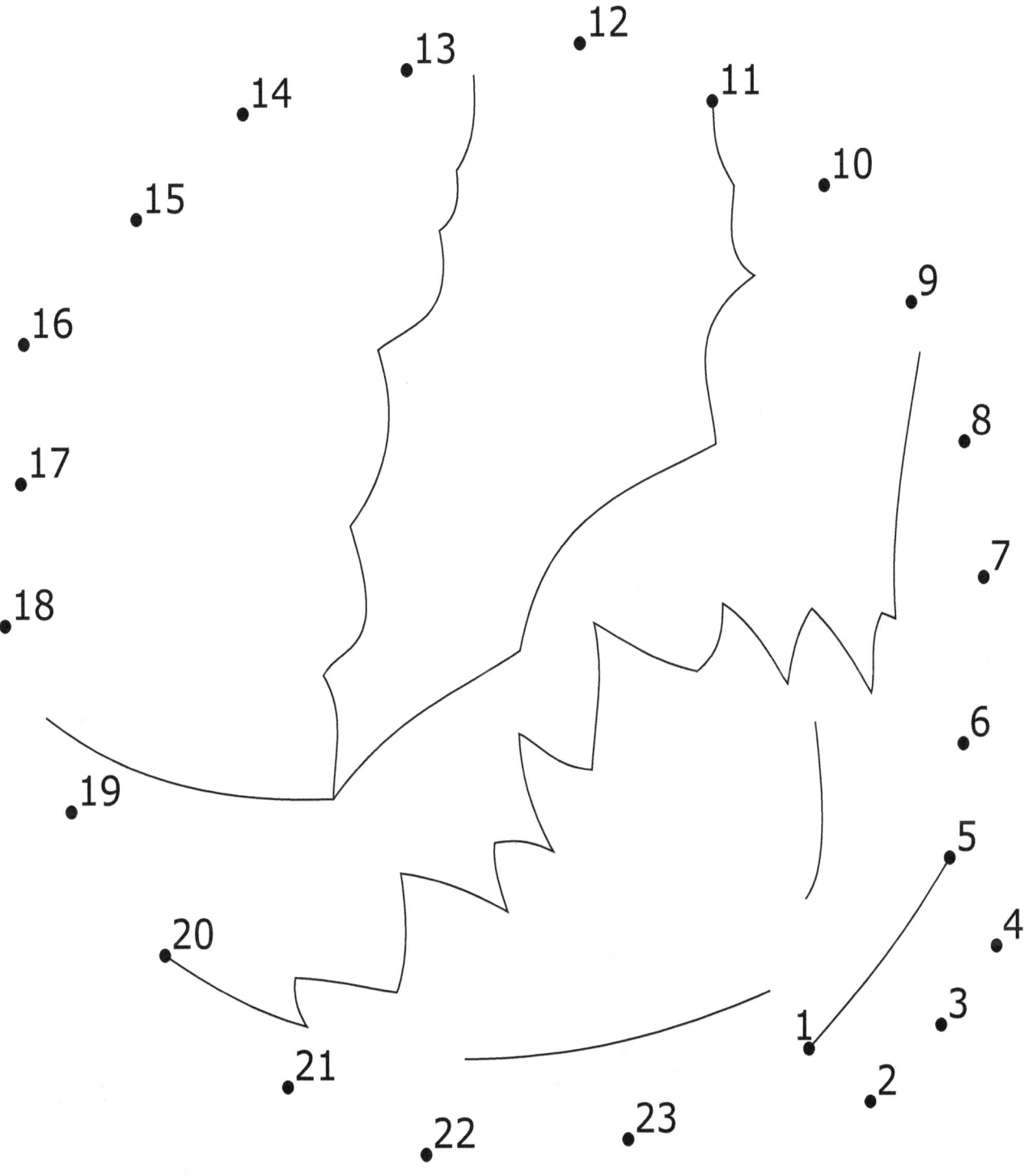

Manager

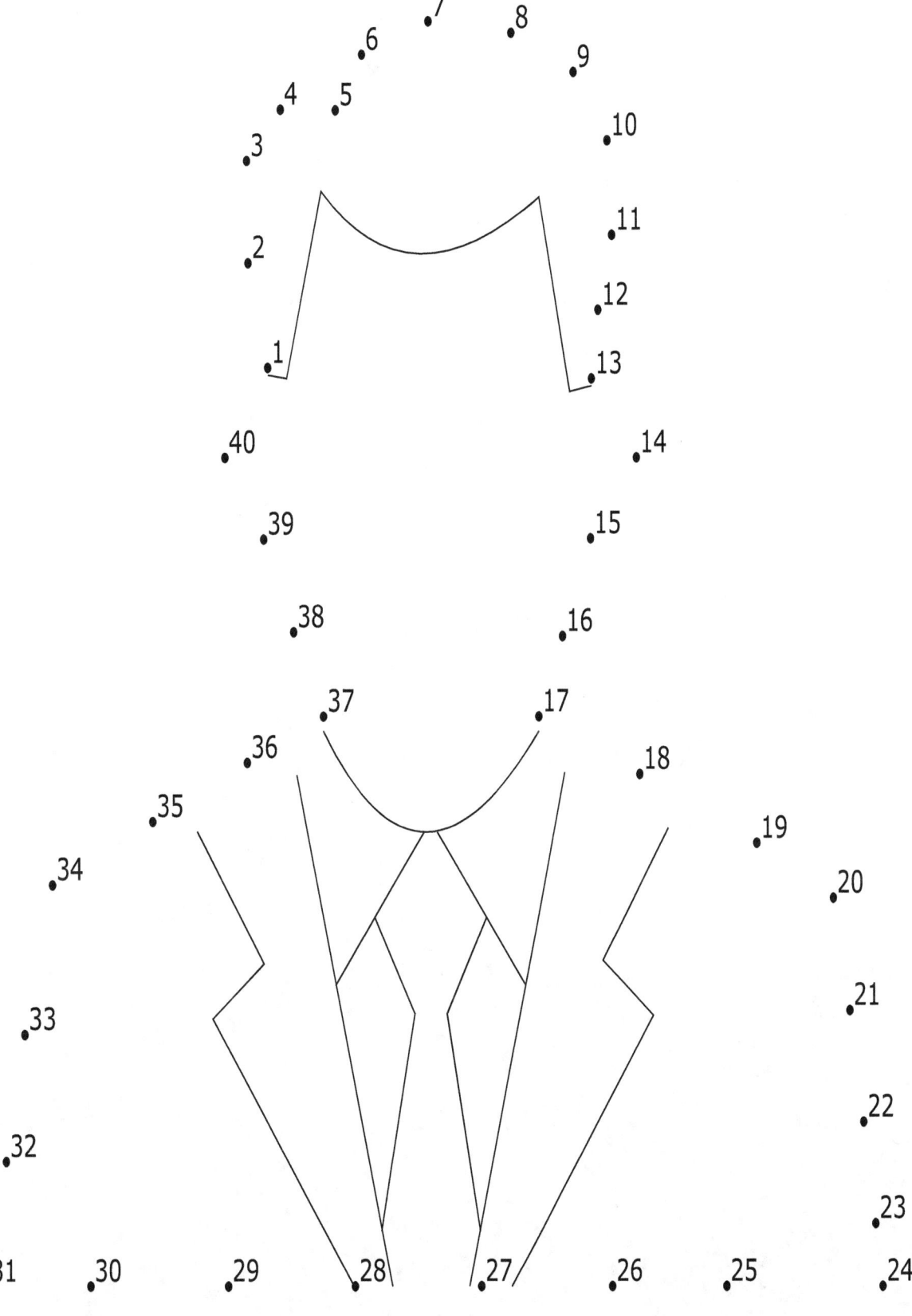

Margarine

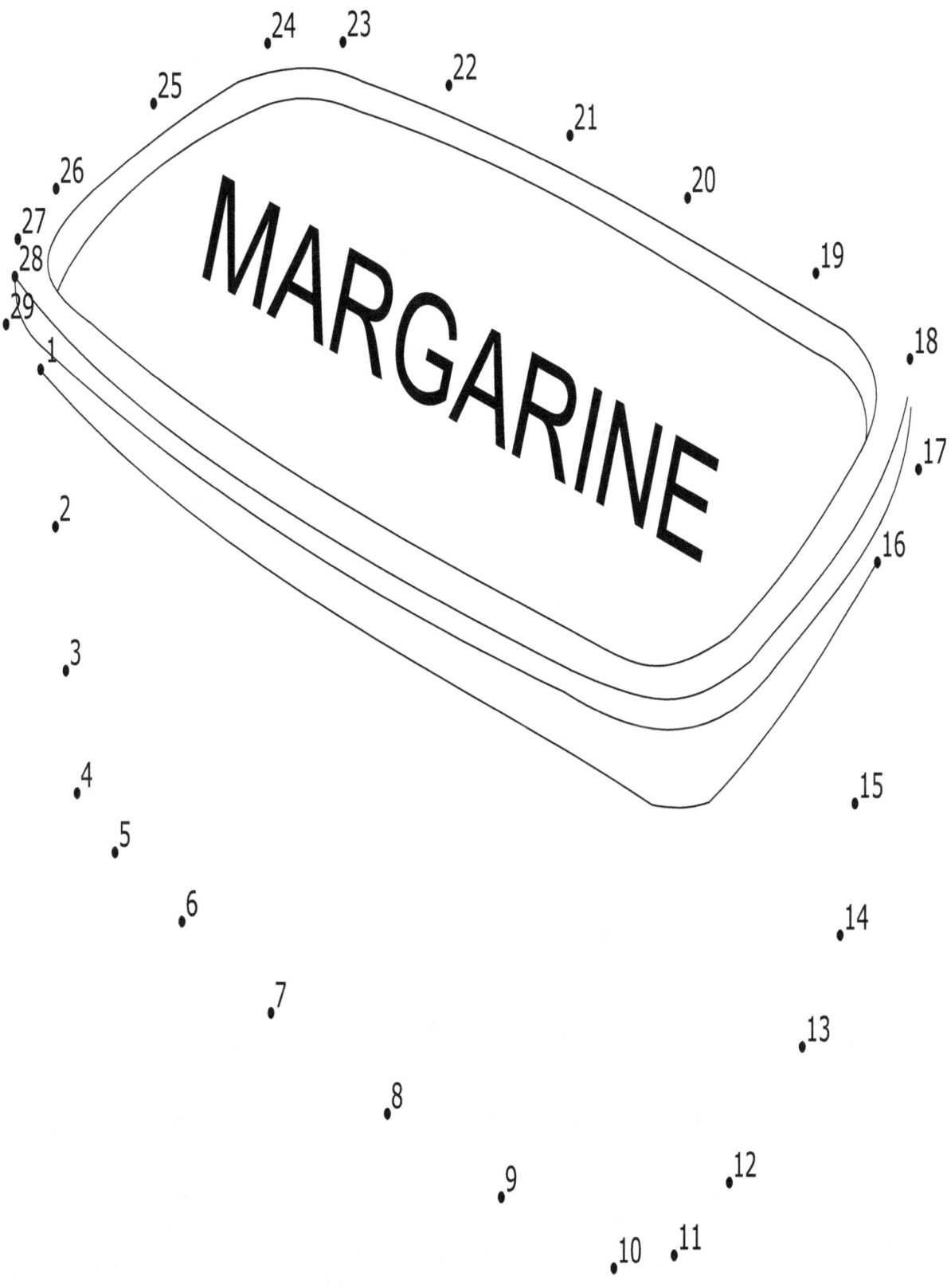

Medicine

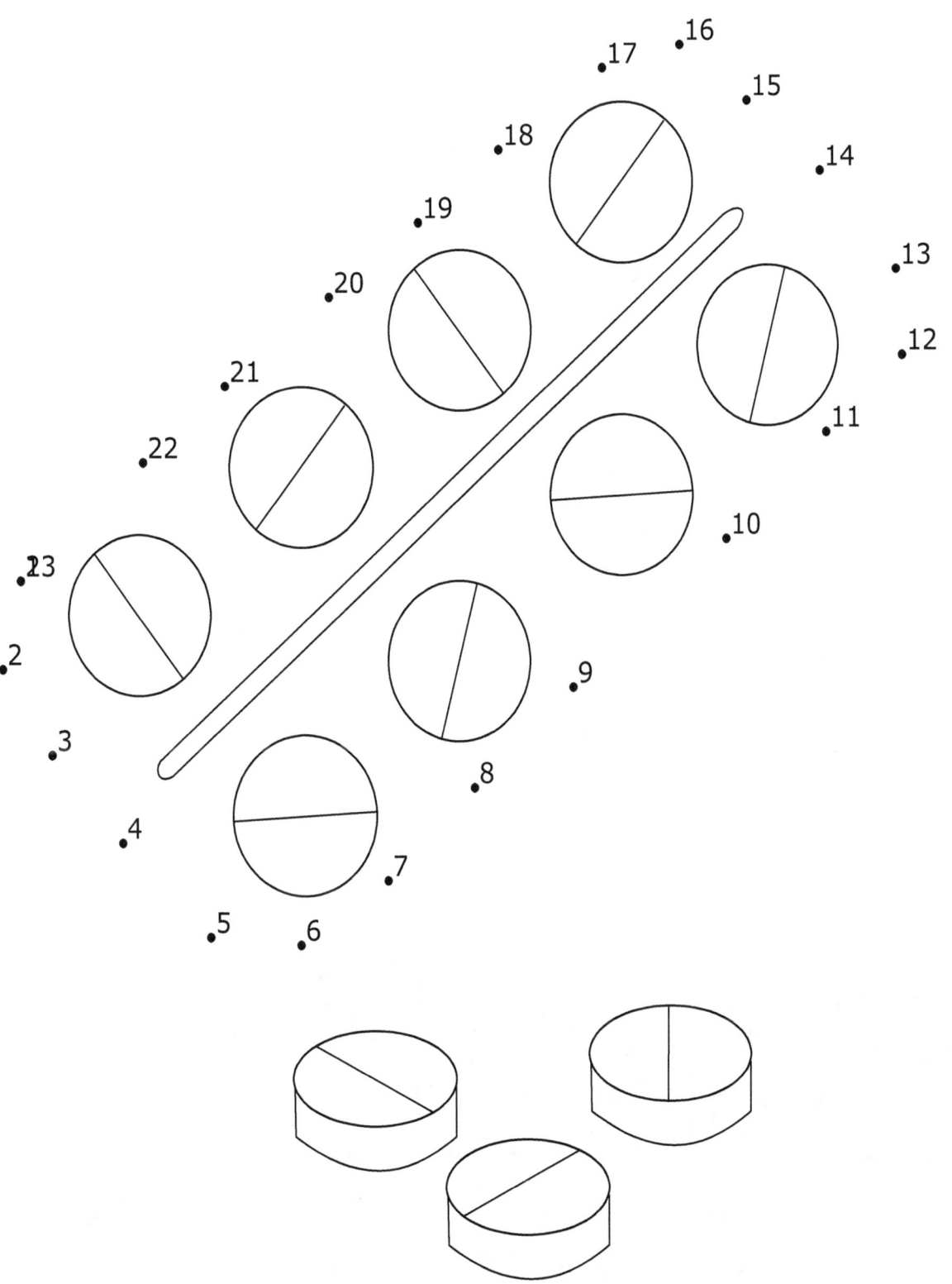

Medicine

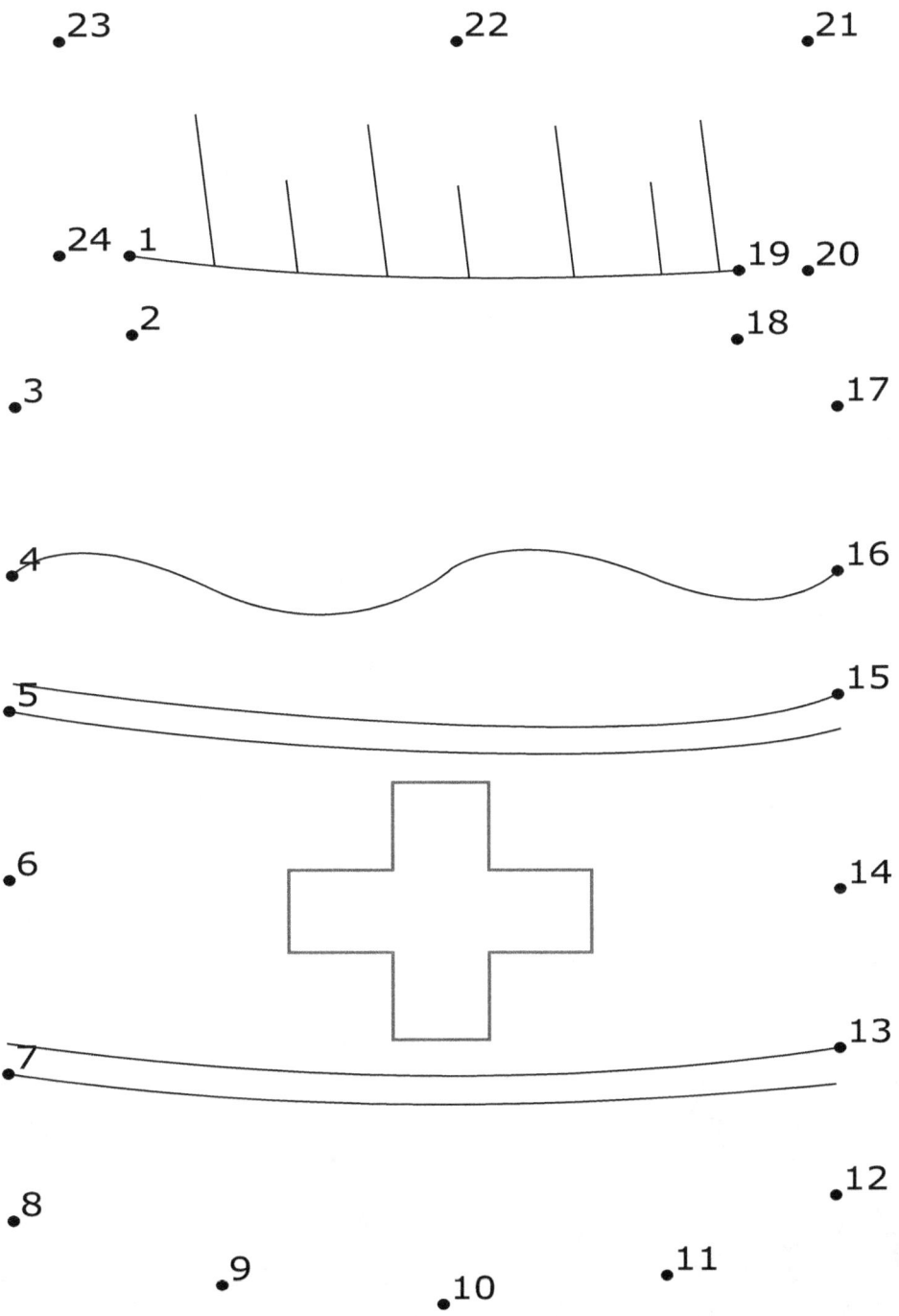

Mushroom

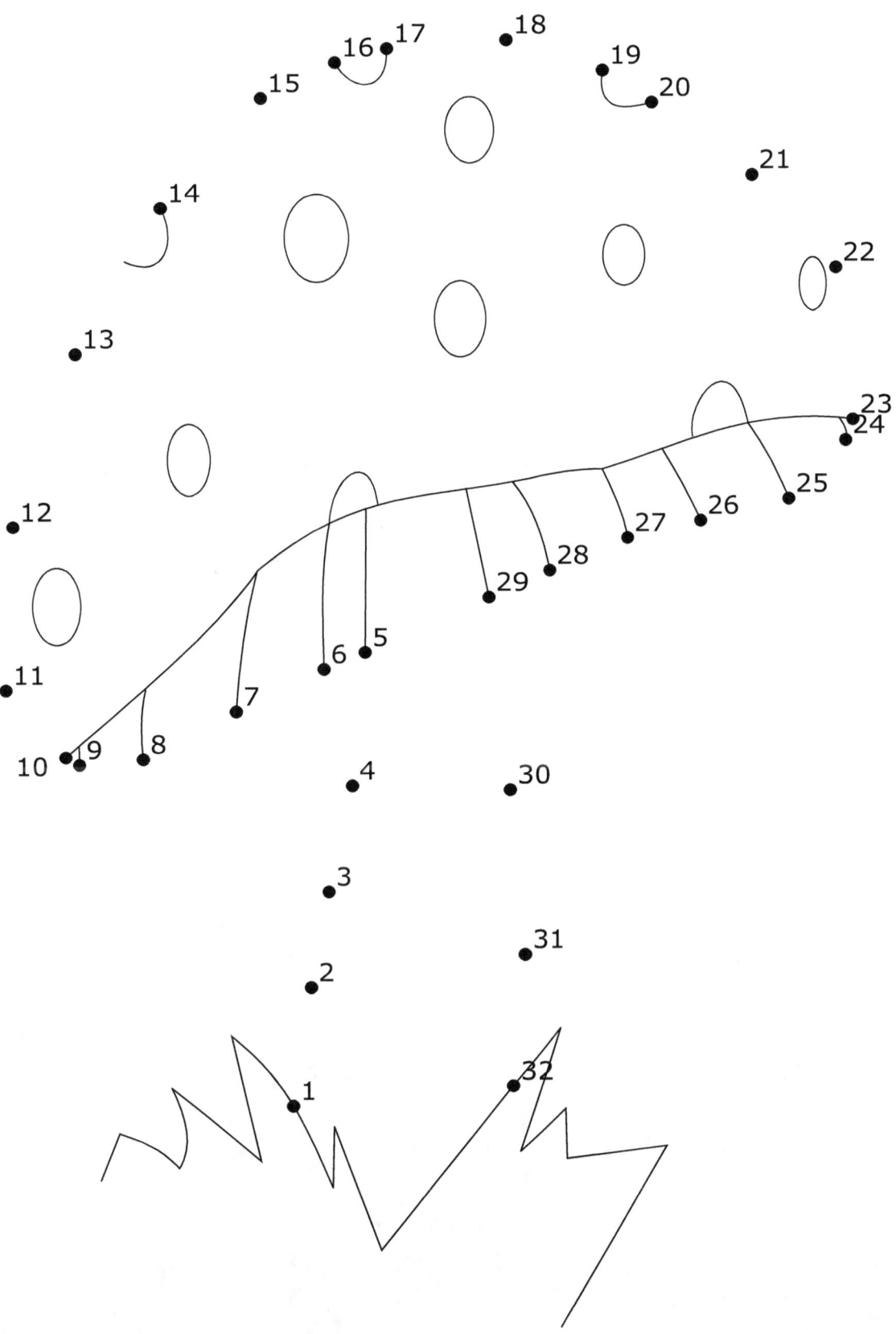

Mushroom

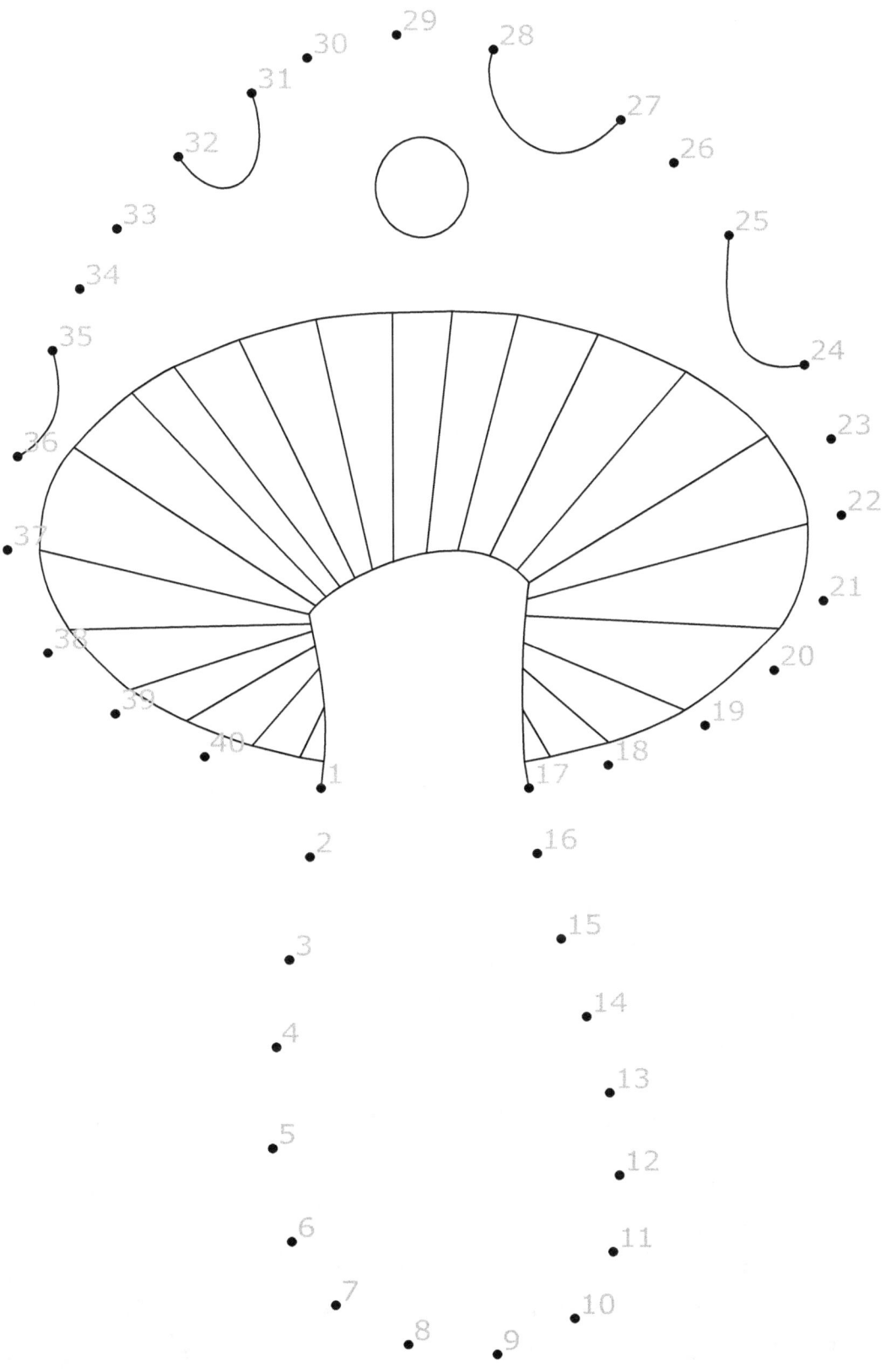

Pineapple

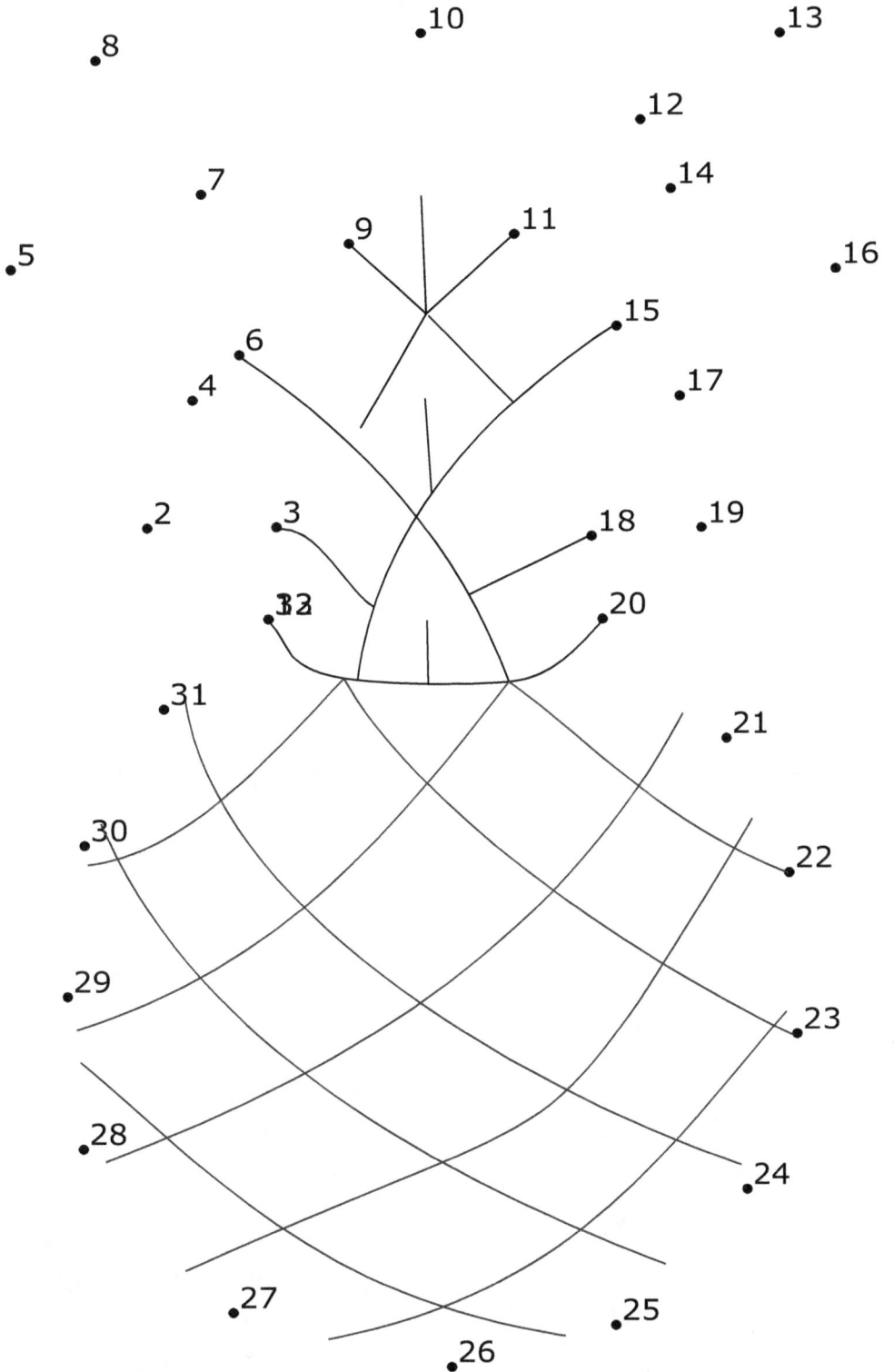

Potato

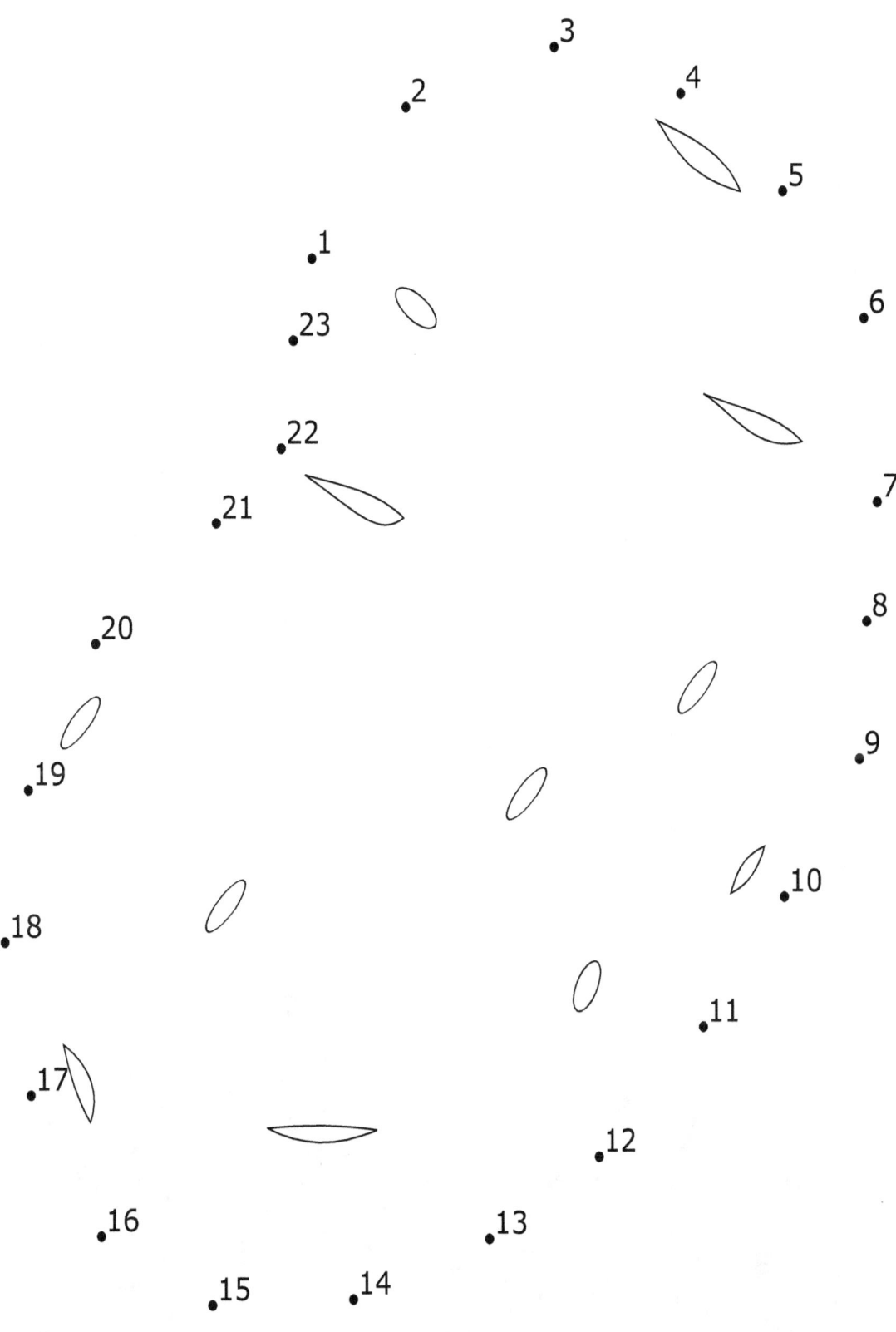

Ready-Meal

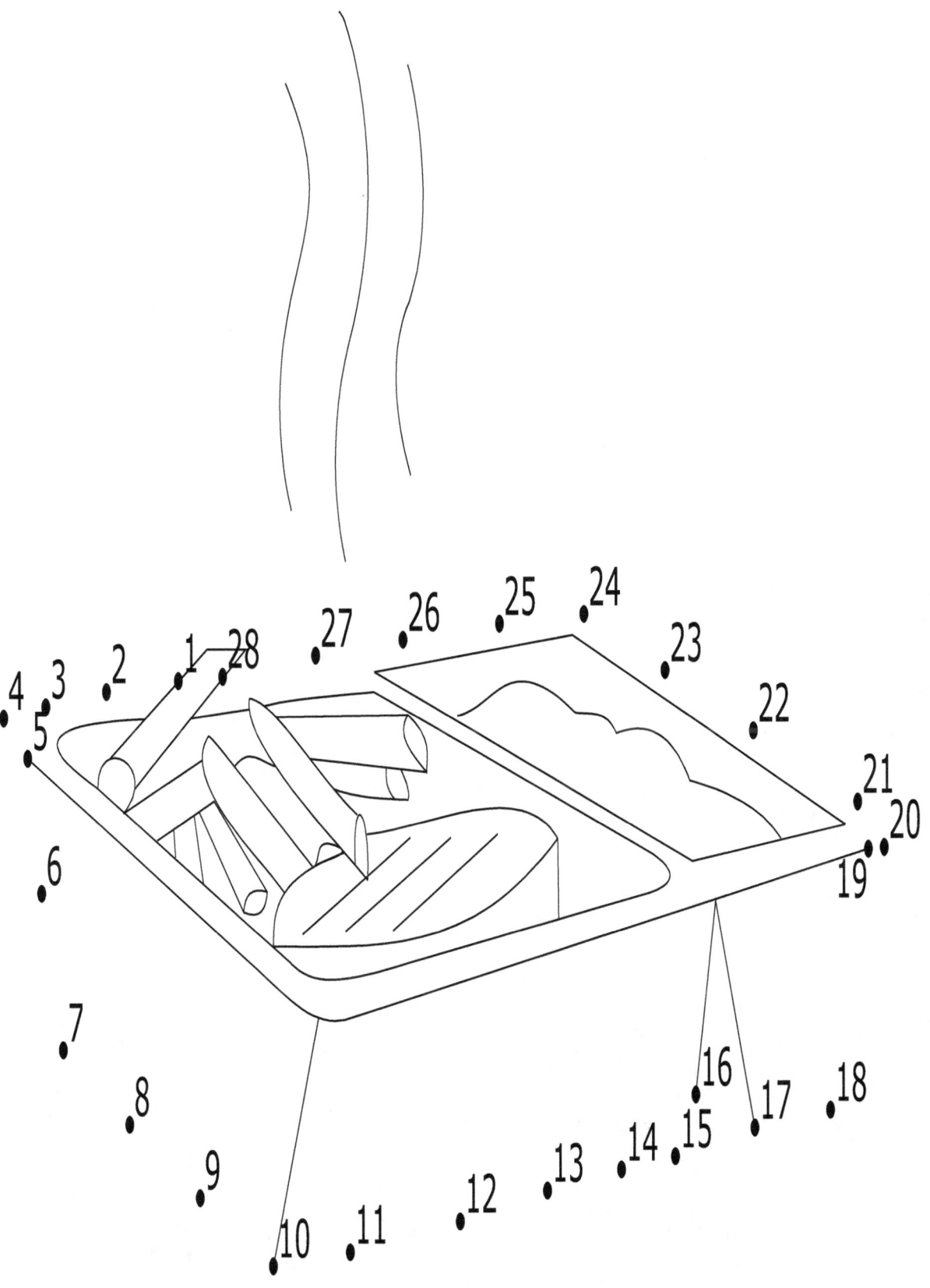

Sponge

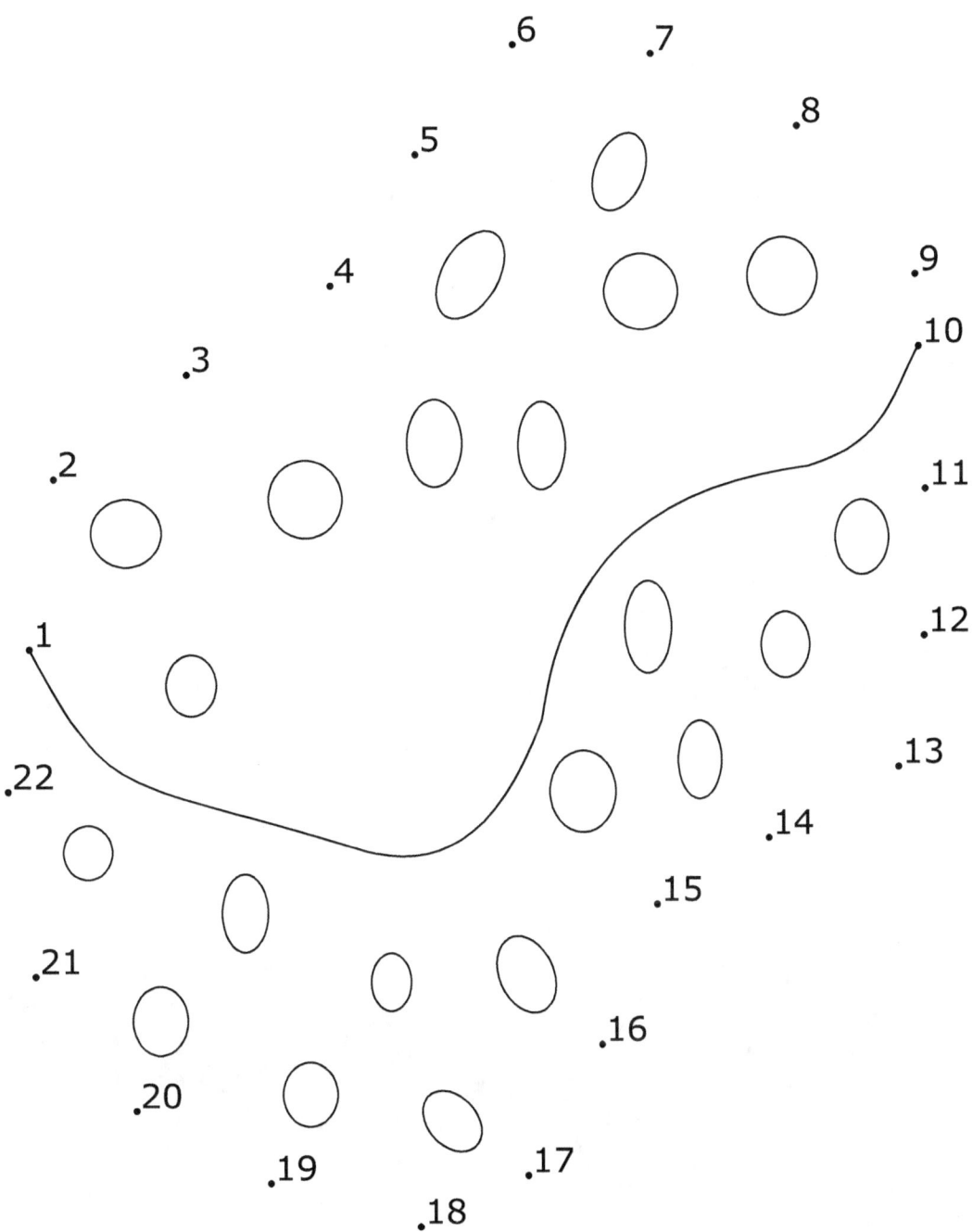

Soup

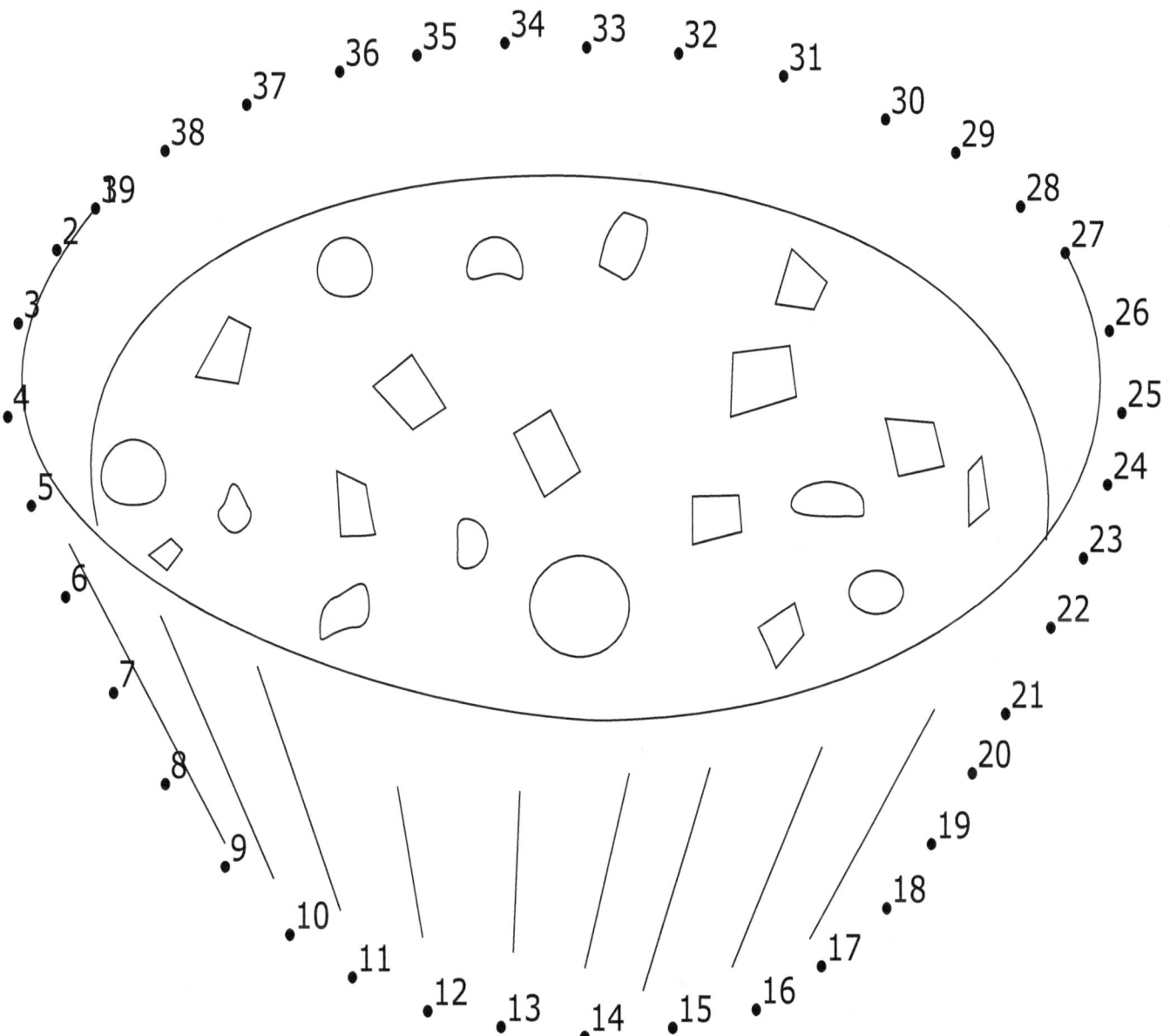

Supermarket

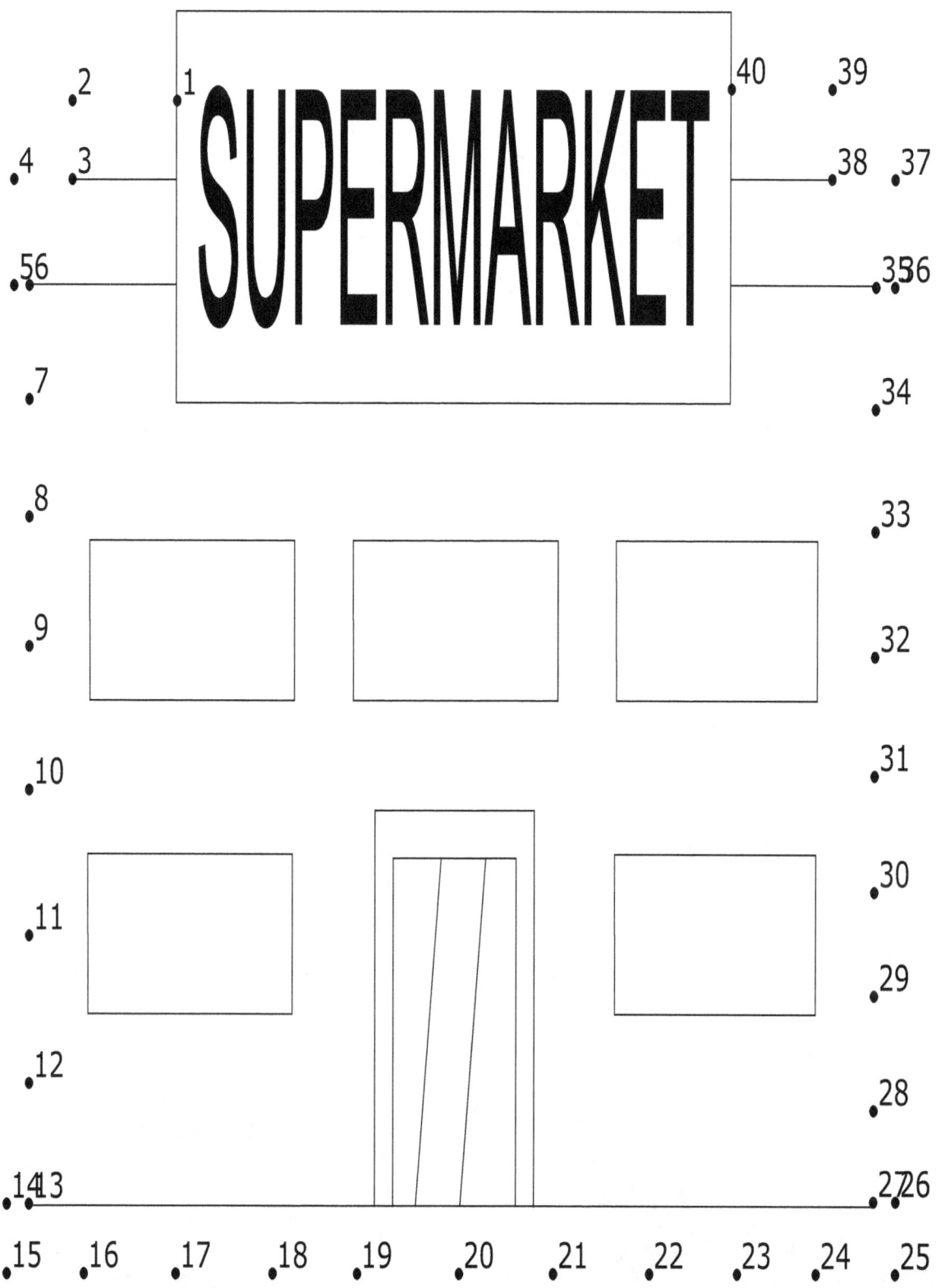

Toothpaste

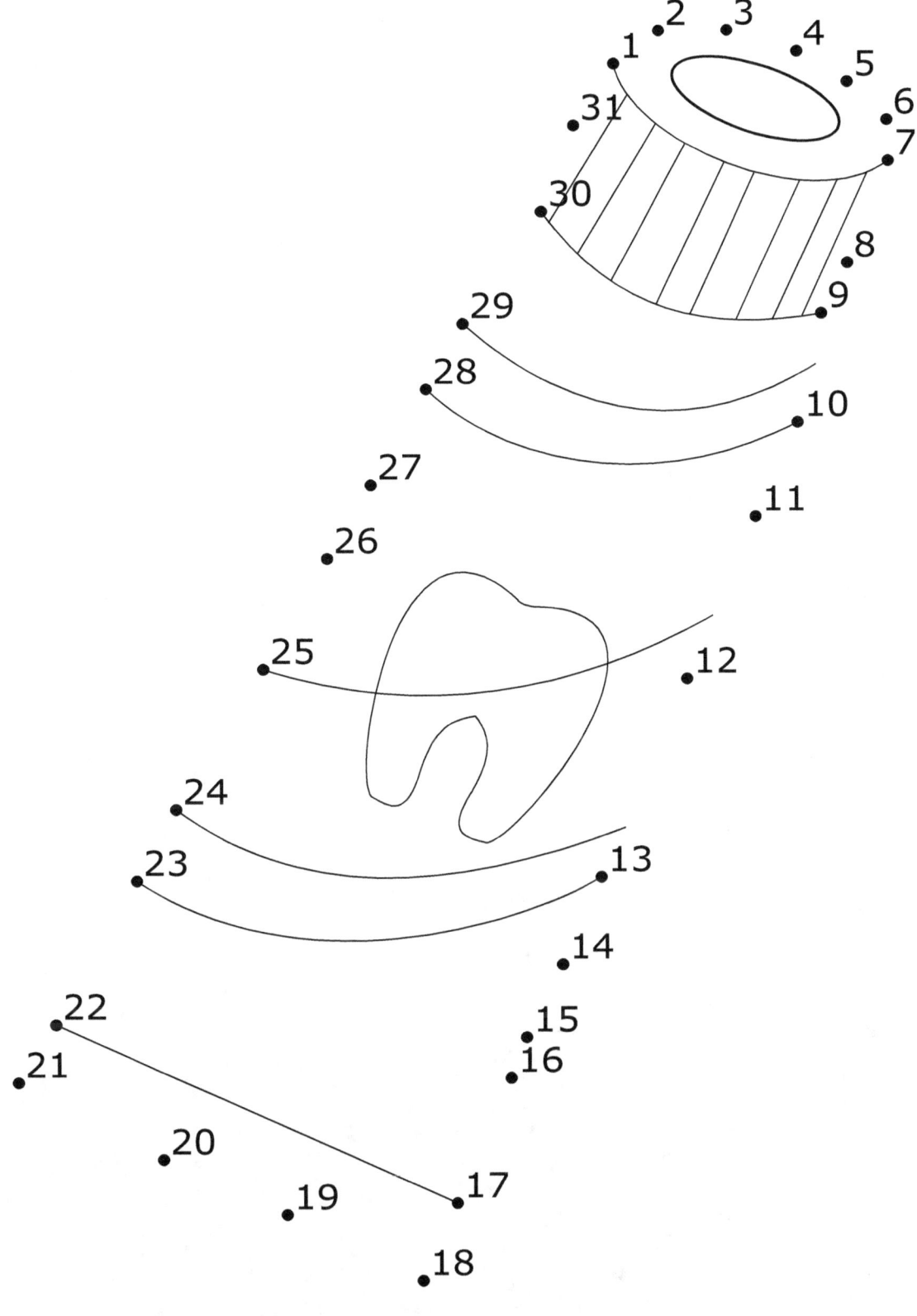

Vegetables

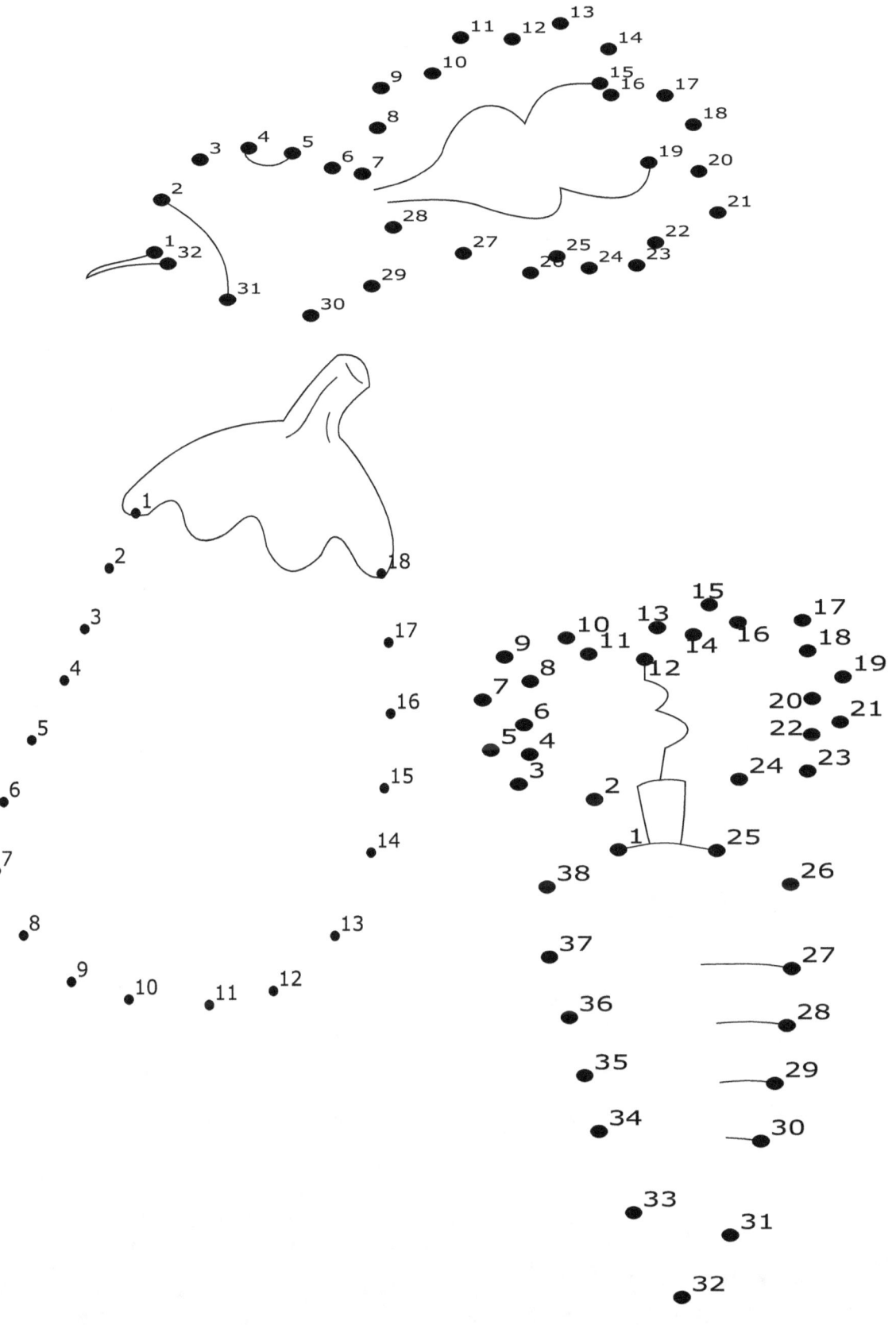

Washing Powder

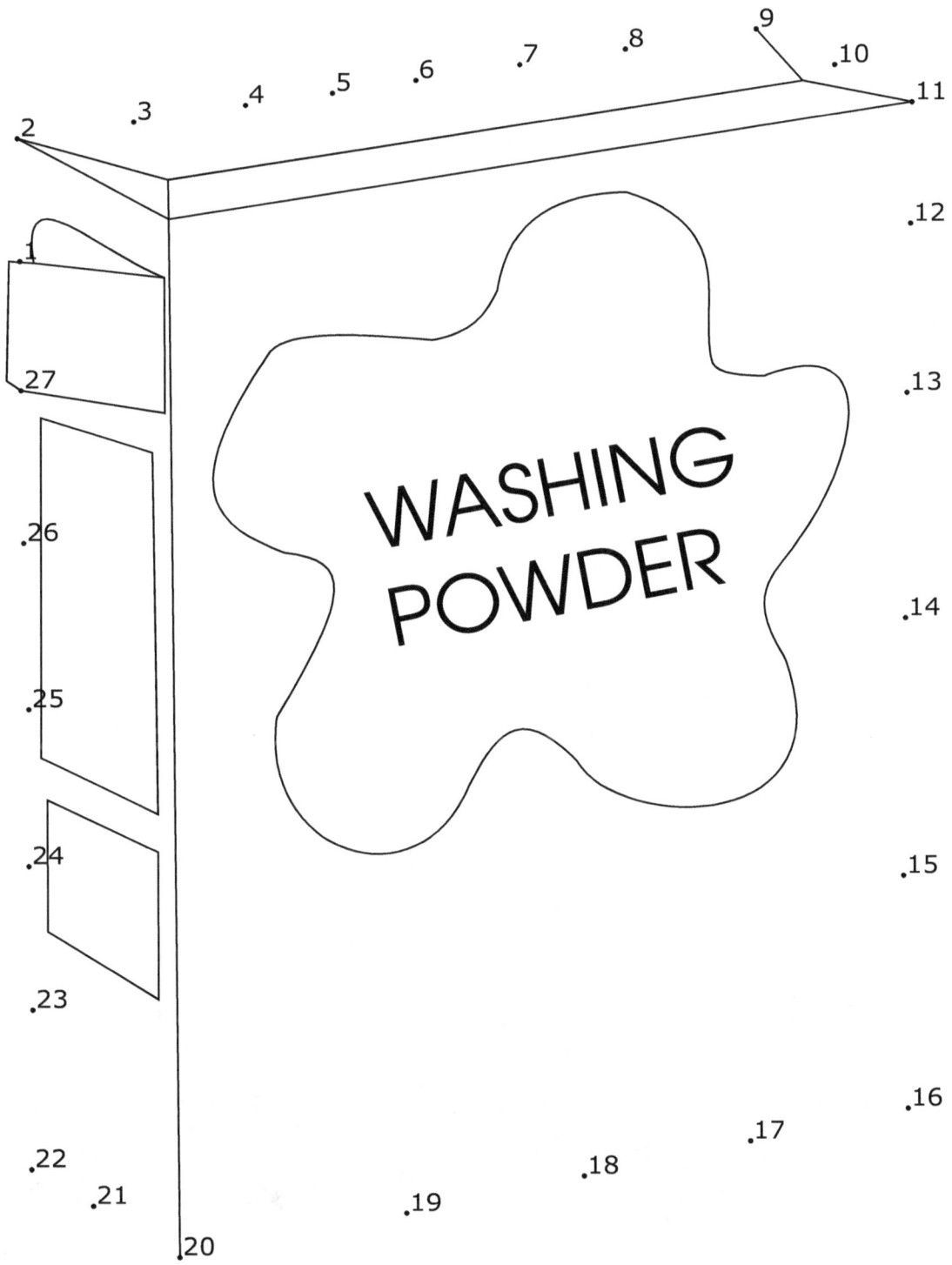

Water Bottle

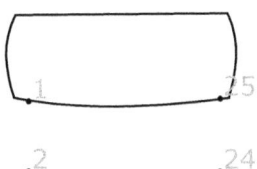
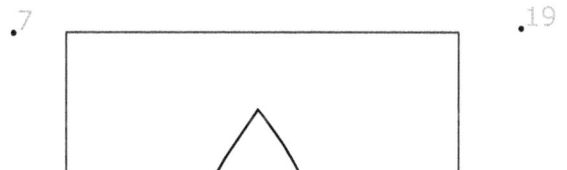

Watermelon

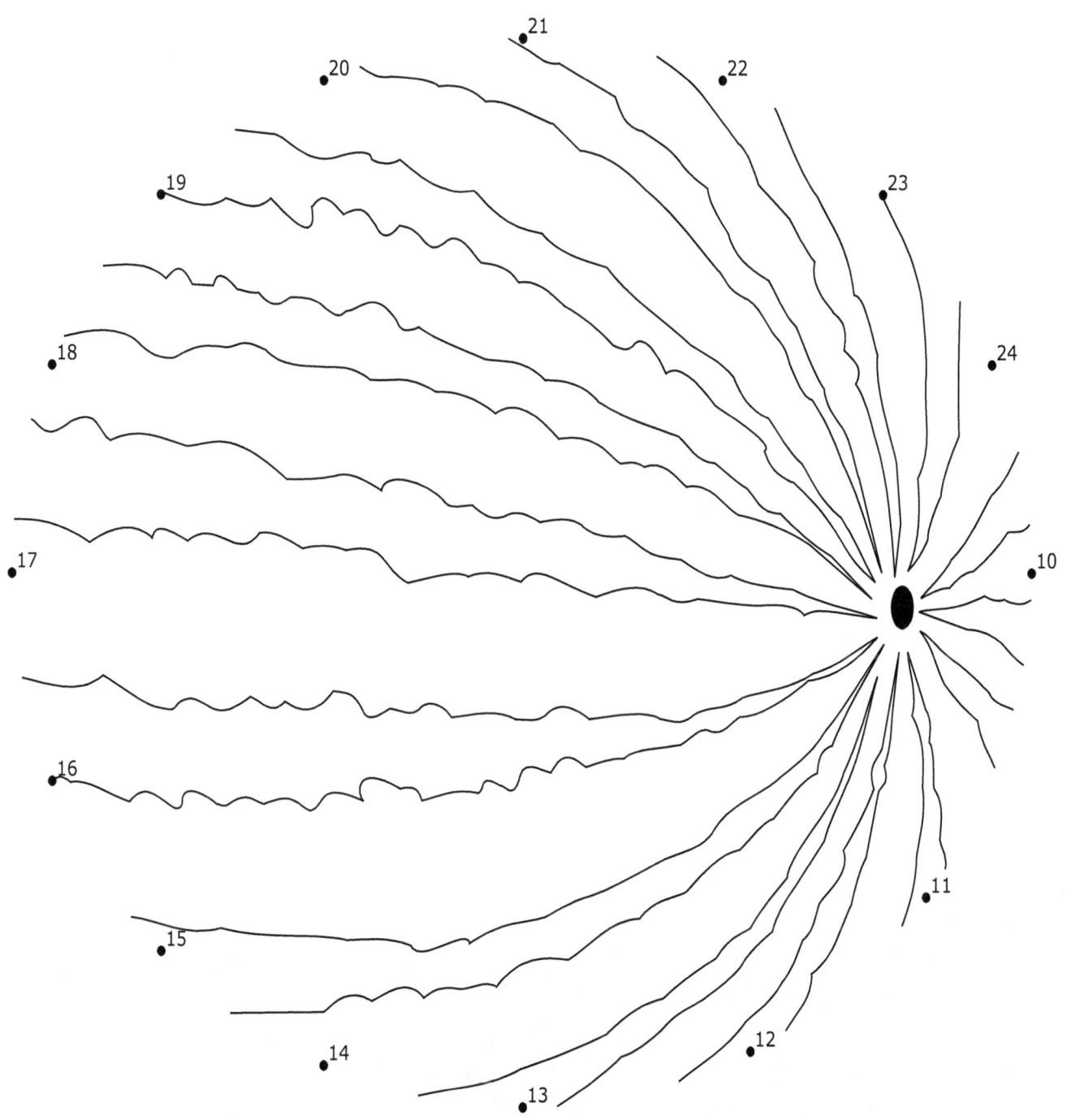

Yogurt

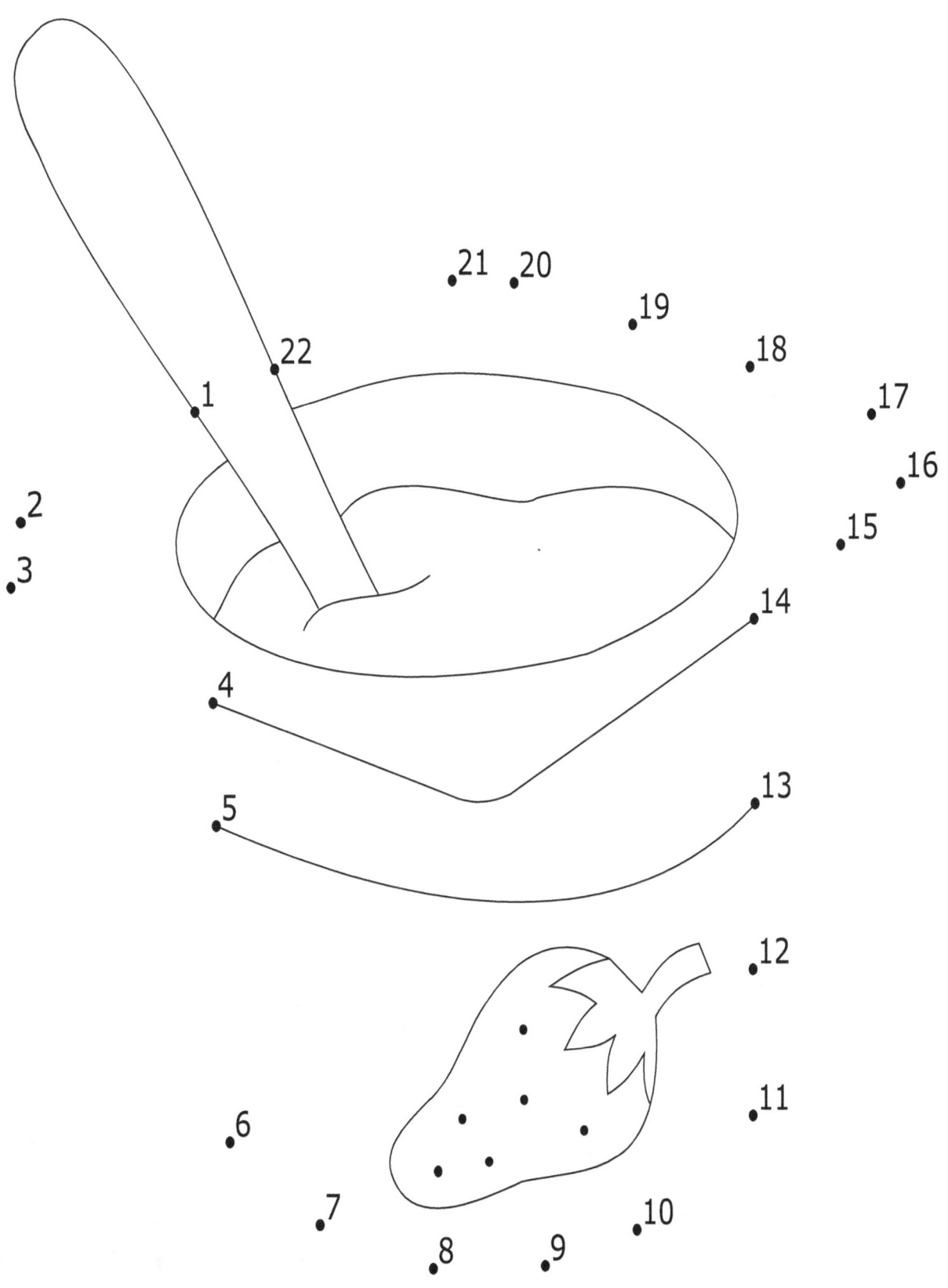

www.ingramcontent.com/pod-product-compliance
Lightning Source LLC
Chambersburg PA
CBHW080503220526
45465CB00006B/2356